A Business Guide to

© *Copyright Law:*

What You Don't

Know

Can Co$t You!

By Woody Young

Joy Publishing
San Juan Capistrano, California

Acknowledgements

The editors would like to thank
Kathy Dongarra and Craig White for their
assistance in compiling, editing and
illustrating this book.

Library of Congress Cataloging-in-Publication Data

Young, Woody
  Copyright Law: What You Don't Know Can Cost You!

Bibliography:p.
1. Copyright—United States. 2. Business and
publishers—United States. I. Title
1944-
KF3020.S78 1988   346.7304'82   88-092557
ISBN 0-939513-70-6   347.306482
ISBN 0-939513-71-4 (pbk.)

Copyright Law: What You Don't Know Can Cost You! ©*1988 Joy Publishing.*
Illustrated drawings ©1986,1987,1988 California Clock Company.
Joy Publishing, 26131 Avenida Aeropuerto, Suite B,
San Juan Capistrano, California 92675.

Italicized text by Woody Young and from Copyright not Copycat: A
Writer's Guide to Copyright, by Sally E. Stuart and Woody Young,
Joy Publishing, used with permission. Other text is taken from,
United States Government materials and is not copyrighted.

Kit-Cat® is a registered trademark of California Clock Company
and is used with permission.

Table of Contents

Questions Most Frequently Asked About Copyright Law

Preface

- *If I have reason to believe that someone has infringed upon a copyright of mine, do I go to the Copyright Office?*

Chapter One

- *What does it mean if I own the copyright on a written work?*
- *What is meant by tangible form?*
- *At what point do I own this copyright?*
- *If copyright is automatic, from the time I created it, and I control its use, how is that copyright transferred to someone else?*
- *What is "work for hire"?*
- *Why do publishers send work-for-hire contracts for regular purchases of articles from free-lance writers?*
- *Should a free-lance writer ever sign a work-for-hire agreement?*
- *Could I be tricked into doing a work for hire without knowing it?*
- *Does the copyright expire at the beginning or end of the last year of coverage?*

Chapter Two

Chapter Three

- *I teach writing classes regularly, and sometimes want to make copies of articles or other material from books or magazines to distribute to my students. I understand it's legal to make multiple copies like that as long as it's for nonprofit, educational purposes.*
- *How do I go about asking for permission? I wouldn't usually have the author's address, so who do I ask? And how do I know if the author or publisher holds the copyright?*
- *What information do I need to send when I ask for permission, and what exactly to I ask for?*
- *Are permissions granted free, or is there a charge for them? If there's a charge, do I pay it or does the publisher?*
- *When do I ask for these permissions— before I sell a book or article, or after?*
- *Do I have to ask permission to use the contents of a letter someone has sent me?*
- *Can I use a small part of a popular song without receiving permission?*
- *Can copyrighted computer programs be used for personal use on more than one computer?*
- *What about business use of copyrighted programs on more than one computer?*
- *Do you have to pay royalty rights to play a radio, TV. or video in a public place?*
- *What are reprints?*
- *Can I make copies for personal use?*
- *Are violations of the copyright warnings a serious offense?*
- *What is an infringement?*
- *Is each infringement considered a separate violation?*

Chapter Four

- *What about reproductions of my work for the blind and handicapped?*

Chapter Five

- *How can I find out who owns a copyright?*
- *Why does a business need to know about copyright?*

Chapter Six

- *In which countries is my copyright honored?*

Chapter Seven

- *If a piece is copyrighted from the time I have it typed, why would I register a copyright?*
- *How does the copyright law define "publication"?*
- *How long do I have to register something?*
- *Do I have to copyright a manuscript before I send it to an editor?*
- *Do I need to register the copyright on a book before I submit it?*
- *Are there any situations in which I am required to register a work before submitting it?*
- *Do I have to wait until a piece is published before I can register the copyright?*
- *If I copyright something when it is unpublished, do I have to do it again once it is published?*
- *What constitutes a collection?*
- *Do I have to send the Library of Congress a copy of my book when it's published?*
- *Do I just write the Copyright Office and ask them to send the copyright registration form?*
- *How much does it cost to register a copyright?*
- *When does my copyright become effective?*
- *I published an article with a copyright notice, but it wasn't registered, and I received a request from the Copyright Office to send them two copies of it. Why is that? Do I have to send the copies?*
- *Why would I want to copyright seminars, programs or speeches?*
- *Are my creative advertisements copyrightable?*
- *Should you copyright newspaper or magazine ads?*

Preface

The Copyright Office is primarily an office of records: a place where claims to copyright are registered when the claimant has complied with the requirements of the copyright law. The Copyright Office furnishes information about the provisions of the copyright law and the procedures for making registration, explains the operations and practices of the Copyright Office, and reports on facts found in the public records of the Office. However, the Regulations of the Copyright Office (Code of Federal Regulations, Title 37, Chapter II) prohibit employees from offering legal advice or opinions.

The Copyright Office cannot do any of the following:

- Comment upon the merits, copyright status, or ownership of particular works, or upon the extent of protection afforded to particular works by the copyright law;
- Compare for similarities copies of works deposited for registration or give opinions on the validity of claims;
- Advise on questions of possible copyright infringement or prosecution of copyright violations;

"Can you help me?"

4

- Draft or interpret contract terms;
- Enforce contracts or recover manuscripts;
- Recommend particular publishers, agents, lawyers, ''song services,'' and the like; or
- Help in getting a work published, recorded, or performed.

Many requests for assistance require professional legal advice, frequently that of a copyright expert. However, even though the Copyright Office cannot furnish services of this kind, its policy is to be helpful in supplying the information and services it is authorized to provide.

If you need information or guidance on legal matters such as disputes over the ownership of a copyright, suits against possible infringers, the procedure for getting a work published, or the method of obtaining royalty payments, it may be necessary to consult an attorney.

For further information about copyrights, call the Copyright Office at **(202) 287-8700.** *To order copyright circulars and forms, write:*

Publications Section, LM-455
Copyright Office
Library of Congress
Washington, DC 20559

The editors of this book have compiled information gleaned from the circulars and forms published by the Copyright Office. No material has been added that would confuse the meaning of these documents. Text in italics has been reworded and/or written by the editors and should not be considered as government publications material.

Our goal is to provide the information you need to know and the forms you need to have to register a copyright. Throughout the book we have indicated which circulars may be referred to for additional information. Should questions arise that are not answered in this book, contact the Copyright Office for more information. All legal matters should be referred to an attorney.

Q: If I have reason to believe that someone has infringed on a copyright of mine, do I go to the Copyright Office with the complaint?
A: No, you will have to see a lawyer.

Introduction

In my extensive involvement with businesses of all kinds, I have found that the area of copyright law is the most confusing, frustrating, and frightening to the average person. Unfortunately, many of them simply try too ignore it in the hopes that it will go away, or that they will never have to deal with it directly.

They couldn't be more wrong. The copyright law is the guardian of all our rights. To not familiarize ourselves with its affect on our business is to jeopardize the protection it was created to afford us. The risks are too great.

It is for that reason that this book has been written. Granted, the law can be baffling for the average person who cares little for the legal-eze that surrounds it, so I have tried to break out those sections that are of most interest and concern to you as a business person. Because there is a danger in adding too much interpretation to a law such as this, I have tried to deviate as little as possible from the original text. However, I have added questions and answers to each section that will help you interpret the law as it applies to you.

When you have a specific question, I suggest that you look it up in the listing of questions at the front of this book, find it in the appropriate chapter, and read the answer. Then, if the Q & A alone does not give sufficient clarification, go on and read the full text of the law that accompanies that section.

Within the content of this book, you will find all you need to know as far as when, where and how to register a copyright, the cost, what protection it affords you, what can and cannot be copyrighted, what constitutes fair use, how to get permission to use other people's material, how to deal with work-for-hire contracts, where to put a copyright notice, and much more. It is a valuable resource you will want to keep handy to answer all the copyright questions that will come up in your day-to-day relations with others.

Please keep in mind, however, that it is not meant to replace the qualified legal advice you will need to deal with specific copyright problems you may encounter. Its purpose is more to answer any general questions that come up, as well as making you more knowledgeable in your dealings with others in business.

You will find that many of the business persons you deal with will not have even a working knowledge of the copyright law or how it applies to your relationship with them. They either are not aware of the changes brought about by the new law that took affect January 1, 1978, or they simply depend on the company's legal office to handle any questions on copyright. For that reason, many of the benefits and protections extended to you will be lost or forfeited if you do not know what your rights are.

I suggest that you study this book until you are aware of your basic rights and obligations, and then keep it handy for reference anytime a new problem or question comes up.

The Copyright Act is not a vague, confusing document meant to mystify and frustrate you. It was created to protect your rights. Basically the new law says that any rights not specifically purchased belong to you, and you will control when and how your material will be used. A working knowledge of the law will better assure that you retain that control.

In closing, you need to be aware that with the copyright law, as with any law, its application and ramifications are always changing to some extent. We know what the law actually says, but we do not always know exactly how it will affect us until court cases dealing with specific points of the law have been settled. For that reason, I suggest that you send your name and address to be put on the mailing list for the Copyright Office. Send to the Information and Publications Section at the address given in the Preface. In that way you will receive any new information of applications of the law that you will need to know about.

As a business person, you have certain legal and ethical responsibilities to other businesses. This book will help you understand and fulfill those responsibilities.

1

Copyright Basics

Q: What does it mean if I own the copyright on a written work?

A: Copyright ownership means that you own and control all rights to it, including the right to make copies, prepare derivative works based on it, distribute it, perform or display it publicly, or sell or transfer it to anyone you choose.

Q: What is meant by tangible form?

A: As soon as your work is down on paper you can put a copyright notice on it.

Q: At what point do I own this copyright?

A: As soon as your work is in tangible form.

Q: If copyright is automatic, from the time I created it, and I control its use, how does that copyright get transferred to someone else?

A: There are a few common ways:

1) *If an editor or publisher buys all or exclusive rights to story or article you write;*

2) *If you transfer a copyright to a friend or relative, for tax purposes, or leave it to someone in your will; and*

3) *If you sell a book, the various subsidiary rights (ie., paperback, movie, and book club rights) can be transferred individually. This will be specified in your book contract.*

4) *If you license a company to use your copyright on their product.*

What is Copyright?

Copyright is a form of protection provided by the laws of the United States (Title 17, *United States Code*) to the authors of "original works of authorship" including

Copyright is protection under the United States law

literary, dramatic, musical, artistic, and certain other intellectual works. This protection is available to both published and unpublished works. Section 106 of the Copyright Act generally gives the owner of copyright the exclusive right to do and to authorize others to do the following:

- To reproduce the copyrighted work in copies or phonorecords;
- To prepare derivative works based upon the copyrighted works;
- To distribute copies or phonorecords of the copyrighted work to the public by sale or other transfer of ownership, or by rental, lease, or lending;
- To perform the copyrighted work publicly, in the case of literary, musical, dramatic, and choreographic works, pantomimes, and motion pictures and other audiovisual works; and
- To display the copyrighted work publicly, in the case of literary, musical, dramatic, and choreographic works, pantomimes, and pictorial, graphic, or sculptural works, including the individual images of a motion picture or other audiovisual work.

It is illegal for anyone to violate any of these rights provided to the owner of copyright by the Act. These rights, however, are not unlimited in scope. Sections 107 through 118 of the Copyright Act establish limitations on these rights. In some cases, these limitations are specified exemptions from copyright liability. One major limitation is the doctrine of "fair use," which is now given a statutory basis by Section 107 of the Act. In other instances, the limitation takes the form of a "compulsory license" under which certain limited uses of copyrighted works are permitted upon payment of specified royalties and compliance with statutory conditions. For further information about the limitations of any of these rights, consult the Copyright Act or write to the Copyright Office.

Who Can Claim Copyright?

Copyright protection subsists from the time the work is created in fixed form *(on paper, for example)*; that is, it is an incident in the process of authorship. The copyright in the work of authorship immediately becomes the property of the author who created it. Only the author or those deriving their rights through the author can rightfully claim copyright.

In the case of works made for hire, the employer and not the employee is considered the author. Section 101 of the copyright statute defines a "work made for hire" as:

1) a work prepared by an employee within the scope of his or her employment; or

2) a work specially ordered or commissioned for use as a contribution to a collective work, as a part of a motion picture or other audiovisual work, as a translation, as a supplementary work, as a compilation, as an instructional text, as a test, as answer material for a test, or as an atlas, if the parties expressly agree in a written instrument signed by them that the work shall be considered a work made for hire.

*Q: **What is "work for hire"?***
A: The work made for hire provision in the copyright law was intended to apply to the writing an employee did for an employer as a part of his job (the writing belongs to the employer, not the employee), or when a writer is contracted to contribute to a collection, motion picture, instructional text, and the like, when they agree in a contract that the work is to be considered work done for hire.

*Q: **Why do publishers send work-for-hire contracts for regular purchases of articles from free-lance writers?***
A: When the new law came into effect in 1978, the work for hire provision appeared to be the only loop-hole publishers could find that would guarantee them all rights to a writer's work, so they tried to use the law in their favor. Fortunately, most legitimate publishers have stopped sending such contracts, primarily because writers stuck together and refused to sign them.

*Q: **Should a free-lance writer ever sign a work-for-hire agreement?***
A: That decision always lies with the author, but most writers don't unless the arrangement with the publisher is genuinely work for hire. For example, an assignment to write curriculum for a publisher that produces Sunday school lessons is often done as work for hire. Also, some writers will sign such a contract if they feel the amount of pay, or prestige, justifies it.

Q: Could I be tricked into doing a work for hire without knowing it?
A: No, a work for hire, as well as the transfer of all rights, has to be agreed to in writing.

The authors of a joint work are co-owners of the copyright in the work, unless there is an agreement to the contrary.

Copyright in each separate contribution to a periodical or other collective work is distinct from copyright in the collective work as a whole and vests initially with the author of the contribution.

Ownership of a book, manuscript, painting, or any other copy or phonorecord does not give the possessor the copyright. The law provides that transfer of ownership of any material object that embodies a protected work does not of itself convey any rights in the copyright. For more information about transfer of copyright, write the Copyright Office.

Minors may claim copyright, but state laws may regulate the business dealings involving copyrights owned by minors. For information on relevant state laws, it would be well to consult an attorney.

Q: Is there an easy rule of thumb to be sure the copyright has expired?
A: Yes, take the current year and subtract 75 (for example: 1988 - 75 = 1913); anything copyrighted that year and before is now in public domain.

Q: Does the copyright expire at the beginning or end of the last year of coverage?
A: All copyrights expire on December 31st of the final year.

Q: How long is a copyright, if you register it?
A: Generally for the author's lifetime, plus 50 years.

Q: What if there are co-authors? How does that affect the length of copyright?
A: The copyright then lasts for 50 years after the last surviving author's death.

Q: How long does the copyright last when the author is anonymous?
A: Then the copyright will be 75 years from publication or 100 years from creation, whichever is shorter.

Length of Copyright Protection

The 1976 law provides that all terms of copyright will run through the calendar year in which they would otherwise expire. This affects not only the duration of copyrights, but also the time limits for renewal registrations. From now on, the last day of a copyright will be December 31 of that copyright's last year; and for works originally copyrighted between 1950 and 1977, all periods for renewal registration will run from December 31 of the 27th year of the copyright and will end on December 31 of the following year.

Works Originally Created on and after January 1, 1978

A work that is created (fixed in tangible form for the first time) on or after January 1, 1978, is automatically protected from the moment of its creation, and is ordinarily given a term enduring for the author's life, plus an additional 50 years after the author's death. In the case of "a joint work prepared by two or more authors who did not work for hire," the term lasts for 50 years after the last surviving author's death. For works made for hire, and for anonymous and pseudonymous works (unless the author's identity is revealed in Copyright Office records), the duration of copyright will be 75 years from publication or 100 years from creation, whichever is shorter.

Works that were created before the present law came into effect, but had neither been published nor registered for copyright before January 1, 1978, have been automatically brought under the statute and are now given federal copyright protection. The duration of copyright in these works will generally be computed in the same way as for works created on or after January 1, 1978: the life-plus-50 or 75/100-year terms will apply to them as well. However, all works in this category are guaranteed at least 25 years of statutory protection. The law specifies that in no case will copyright in a work of this sort expire before December 31, 2002, and if the work is published before that date the term may be extended by another 25 years, through the end of 2027.

"Just how long does a copyright last?"

Works Originally Copyrighted before 1950 and Renewed before 1978

These older works have automatically been given a longer copyright term. Under the statute, copyrights that had already been renewed and were in their second term at any time between December 31, 1976, and December 31, 1977, inclusive, do not need to be renewed again. They were automatically extended to last for a total term of 75 years (a first term of 28 years plus a renewal term of 47 years) from the end of the year in which they were originally secured.
Note: This extension applies not only to copyrights less than 56 years old, but also to older copyrights that had previously been extended in duration under a series of Congressional enactments beginning in 1962. As in the case of all other copyrights subsisting in their second term between

December 31, 1976, and December 31, 1977, inclusive, these copyrights will expire at the end of the calendar year in which the 75th anniversary of the orginal date of copyright occurs.

Q: I started writing in 1976, but didn't have anything published or copyrighted at that time. Does that material have any copyright protection?
A: Anything that was created before the new law took effect (January 1, 1978) is automatically protected. In most cases it gets the same life-plus-50 coverage but no less than 25 years. If it is published before the end of that first 25 years, the copyright will be extended for a second 25 years.

Q: What happened to works that were in the middle of those copyrights when the new law became effective?
A: If a work was copyrighted before 1950 and renewed before 1978, the copyright was automatically extended to last a total of 75 years. If it was first copyrighted after January 1, 1950, but before the new law took effect, the copyright has to be renewed to get an additional 47 years of protection (75 years total). If it is not renewed at the proper time, the protection ends there, and the copyright owner permanently loses the additional 47 years.

Q: How long did copyrights last before the new law took effect?
A: Works could be copyrighted for 28 years and then renewed for another 28 years, for a total of 56 years.

The copyright "lives" on
for 50 years after the author's death

Works Originally Copyrighted between January 1, 1950, and December 31, 1977

Copyrights in their first 28-year term on January 1, 1978, will still have to be renewed in order to be protected for the second term. If a valid renewal registration is made at the proper time, the second term will last for 47 years (19 years longer than the 28-year renewal term under the old law). However, if renewal registration for these works is not made within the statutory time limits, a copyright originally secured between 1950 and 1977 will expire on December 31st of its 28th year, and protection will be lost permanently.

Example: A work copyrighted in 1976 will be eligible for renewal in 2004. If renewed, it will be protected until 2051, but if renewal registration is not made at the proper time, copyright protection will expire permanently at the end of 2004.

For further information about the time limits and other requirements for renewal registration, write for Circular 15, "Renewal of Copyright." For specific information about the extension of copyright terms for works already under statutory protection before 1978, write for Circular R15t "Extension of Copyright Terms."

Q: What does it mean when a work goes into "public domain"?

A: Anytime a piece is published without copyright protection, or the copyright has expired, it is said to have gone into public domain. What that means is that the public may use, without fee, anything that is in public domain. Some documents, like United States Government publications, are not copyrighted, which means they are automatically in public domain (which makes them an excellent research source).

Q: If something goes into public domain— either because it was published without the notice, or the copyright has expired—is there any way to restore the copyright?

A: No, not in that form. All you can do is rewrite the material into a new piece and copyright it in the new form.

What Material is Copyrightable?

Copyright protection exists for "original works of authorship" when they become fixed in a tangible form of expression. The fixation does not need to be directly perceptible, so long as it may be communicated with the aid of a machine or device. Copyrightable works include the following categories:

1) literary works;

2) musical works, including any accompanying words;

3) dramatic works, incuding any accompanying music;

4) pantomimes and choreographic works;

5) pictorial, graphic, and sculptural works;

6) motion pictures and other audiovisual works; and

7) sound recordings.

"Can I copyright all this?"

This list is illustrative and is not meant to exhaust the categories of copyrightable works. These categories should be viewed quite broadly so that, for example, computer programs and most "compilations" are registrable as "literary works"; maps and architectural blueprints are registrable as "pictorial, graphic, and sculptural works."

Cartoons and comic strips generally are among the types of works of authorship protected by copyright. This protection extends to any copyrightable pictorial or written expression contained in the work. The title of a cartoon or comic strip is not subject to copyright protection; neither is the general theme for a cartoon or comic strip, nor the general idea or name for the characters depicted. Titles and names may sometimes be protected under state law doctrines or trademark laws, but this type of protection has nothing to do with the copyright statute.

Not copyrightable

What is not Protected by Copyright?

Material not subject to copyright and for which applications for registration cannot be entertained:

1) Words and short phrases such as names, titles, and slogans; familiar symbols or designs; mere variations of typographic ornamentation, lettering or coloring; mere listing of ingredients or contents;

2) Ideas, plans, methods, systems, or devices, as distinguished from the manner in which they are expressed or described in a writing;

3) Blank forms, such as time cards, graph paper, account books, diaries, bank checks, scorecards, address books, report forms, order forms and the like, which are designed for recording information and do not in themselves convey information;

4) Works consisting entirely of information that is common property containing no original authorship, such as, for example: standard calendars, height and weight charts, tape measures and rulers, schedules of sporting events, and lists or tables taken from public documents or other common sources.

Q: Can products be copyrighted?
A: Yes, if it is a Visual Arts product; but the process which is used to create the product falls under the Patents laws.

Q: What is meant by the term Visual Arts?
A: Examples of three-dimensional Visual Art objects include toys, sculpture, jewelry, artwork applied to T-shirts or onto plates, and fabric or textile attached to or part of such objects. Examples of two-dimensional Visual Arts objects include fabric emblems, decals, greeting cards and picture postcards, maps, drawings, and paintings.

Q: What is a patent?
A: Patents are granted for new ideas, processes, inventions, etc. for usually 17 years by the Patent Office, but usually are not renewable.

Q: Are games, puzzles, etc. able to be copyrighted?
A: Yes, the game board and directions are, but the idea can only be patented. Puzzles with original design artwork are copyrightable.

Q: Are databases copyrightable?
A: Databases may be considered copyrightable as a form of compilations, which are defined in the law as works "formed by the collection and assembling of pre-existing materials or of data that are selected, coordinated, or arranged in such a way that the resulting work as a whole constitutes an original work of authorship." For a more detailed explanation, write to the Copyright Office and request Circular R65.

Q: What is a Trademark?
A: A mark used to identify a product offered to customers and may be registered with the Patent Office and is renewable.

Q: What is a Service Mark?
A: A mark used to identify a service offered to customers, and may be registered with the Patent Office and is renewable.

Q: What is the difference between trademark or service mark and copyright?
A: Trademark registration is handled by the U.S. Patent and Trademark Office. The Copyright Office has no authority in trademark matters. Copyright registration cannot be made for names, titles, and other short phrases or expressions. In general the Federal Trademark statue covers trademarks, service marks, and works, names or symbols that identify or are capable of distinguishing goods or services.

For information about trademark registration you should write to the Commissioner of Patents and Trademarks, Washington, D.C. 20231.

As soon as it's on paper it's copyrighted.

"These can't be copyrighted?"

Q: Should you copyright product cards or product packaging?
A: Yes, especially if they have an unique design, shape or creative form.

Q: I saw another book with the same title as mine. Isn't the title of my book copyrighted?
A: No, titles cannot usually be copyrighted.

Q: I write how-to, craft articles for children, and have seen the same craft ideas in a dozen different magazines. Aren't those articles copyrighted?
A: The articles themselves are, but the ideas contained in the articles are not. Ideas cannot be copyrighted, only the way a particular author describes the process. You may use the same idea in your writing as long as you describe the process differently.

Example: An author writes a book explaining a new system for food processing. The copyright in the book, which comes into effect at the moment the work is fixed in a tangible form, will prevent others from publishing the text and illustrations describing the author's ideas for machinery, processes, and merchandising methods. However, it will not give the author any rights against others who adopt the ideas for commercial purposes, or who develop or use the machinery, processes, or methods described in the book.

Q: Are jokes copyrightable?
A:No, because they would have to be original and few are.

Names, titles, and short phrases or expressions are not subject to copyright protection. Even if a name, title, or short phrase is novel, distinctive, or lends itself to a play on words, it cannot be protected by copyright. The Copyright Office cannot register claims to exclusive rights in brief combinations of words, such as:

1) Names of products or services;

2) Names of businesses, organizations, or groups (including the name of a group of performers);

3) Names or pseudonyms of individuals (including a pen name or stage name);

4) Titles of works;

5) Catchwords, catch phrases, mottoes, slogans, or short advertising expressions;

6) Mere listings of ingredients, as in a recipe or formula; however, when a recipe or formula is accompanied by substantial literary expression in the form of explanation or directions, or when there is a compilation of recipes, there may be a basis for copyright protection.

Ideas, methods, or systems are not subject to copyright protection. Copyright protection therefore is not available for: ideas or procedures for doing, making, or building things; scientific or technical methods or discoveries; business operations or procedures; mathematical principles; formulas; algorithms; or any other sort of concept, process, or method of operation.

14

In order to be protected by copyright, a work must contain at least a certain amount of original literary, pictorial, or musical expression. Copyright does not extend to names, titles, and short phrases or clauses such as column headings or simple check-lists. The format, arrangement, or typography of a work is not protected. Furthermore, copyright protection does not extend to works consisting entirely of information that is common property containing no original authorship.

It is only the actual expression of the author that can be protected by copyright. The ideas, plans, methods, or systems described or embodied in a work are not protected by copyright. Thus, there would be no way to secure copyright protection for the idea or principle behind a blank form or similar work, or for any of the methods or systems involved in it.

An original literary or pictorial work is subject to copyright registration even though it is published in conjunction with a blank form or other material not protected by copyright, provided that the requirements of the copyright law have been met. However, copyright in such a case would extend protection only to the original literary or pictorial expression used by the author, as distinguished from the blank form or other unprotected aspects of the work.

Example: Original photographs published in conjunction with a blank form, or a "compilation of terms or phrases."

Works by the United States Government are not subject to copyright protection. Whenever a work is published in copies or phonorecords consisting preponderantly of one or more works of the United States Government, the notice of copyright shall also include a statement that identifies one or the other of the following: those portions protected by the copyright law or those portions that constitute United States Government material.

*Q: **Do I need to supply a publisher with a Library of Congress catalog number?***
A: No, that will be taken care of by the publisher. However, if you are self-publishing your material, you will have to check the Cataloging in Publication regulations to see if you qualify for the program.

Cataloging in Publication Program

Copyright information is found on the title page of a book as is Cataloging in Publication (CIP) information. The CIP program enables publishers to obtain the Library of Congress catalog information before the book is printed. The catalog information is used by librarians and archivists to order books.

CIP information has no effect on copyright registration; the catalog number is assigned by the Library of Congress, not the Copyright Office.

If you are a publisher and wish to participate in this program, write to:

> ***CIP Office***
> ***Library of Congress***
> ***Washington, DC 20540***

*and request the forms: "Cataloging in Publication— Information for Participating Publishers" and "Publisher's Response." You may also request these forms by telephone, **(202) 287-6372**.*

NOTES:

2 More Copyright Basics

Q: What is a copyright notice?

A: *Copyright notice requires three elements:*
1) The copyright symbol © (C in a circle), the word "copyright," or the abbreviation "Copr.";
2) The year date of first publication (or creation when it has not yet been published); and
3) The name of the owner of copyright (your name if you wrote it).

Notice of Copyright

When a work is published under the authority of the copyright owner, a notice of copyright should be placed on all publicly distributed copies and on all publicly distributed phonorecords of sound recordings. This notice is required even on works published outside the United States. Failure to comply with the notice requirement can result in the loss of certain additional rights otherwise available to the copyright owner.

The use of the copyright notice is the responsibility of the copyright owner and does not require advance permission from, or registration with, the Copyright Office. As mentioned above, use of the notice makes the unpublished works subject to mandatory deposit requirements. For more information about deposits, see chapter 7.

Form of Notice for Visually Perceptible Copies

The notice of visually perceptible copies should contain all of the following three elements:

1) The symbol © (the letter C in a circle),

"What does this stand for?"

or the word "Copyright," or the abbreviation "Copr."; and

2) The year of first publication of the work. In the case of compilations or derivative works incorporating previously published material, the year date of first publication of the compilation or derivative work is sufficient. The year date may be omitted where a pictorial, graphic, or sculptural work, with accompanying textual matter, if any, is reproduced in or on greeting cards, postcards, stationery, jewelry, dolls, toys, or any useful article; and

3) The name of the owner of the copyright in the work, or an abbreviation by which the name can be recognized, or a generally known alternative designation of the owner.

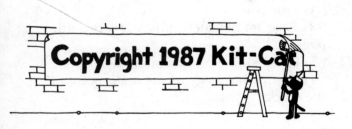

Example: © **1985 John Doe**

The "C in a circle" notice is required only on "visually perceptible" copies." Certain kinds of works, for example, musical, dramatic, and literary works, may be fixed not in "copies" but by means of sound in an audio recording. Since audio recordings such as audio tapes and phonograph disks are "phonorecords" and not "copies,"

Q: Where do you put a copyright notice on a manuscript you are submitting for publication?

A: For a book manuscript, put it on the title page. For a periodical manuscript, put it on the first page, either under your name and address in the upper left corner, or under rights offered and word length in the upper right corner. It always needs to be displayed in a place where it is readily visible.

Q: How do I know if a magazine is copyrighted?

A: If a magazine is copyrighted (and most are), a copyright notice will usually appear on the masthead. If it isn't, a notice to that effect will usually be on the masthead also. Market books often note those periodicals that are not copyrighted.

Q: Do I have to tell the publisher to carry the copyright notice on my piece when it's published in his magazine?

A: If the magazine is copyrighted, you will have automatic protection under the umbrella of the magazine's copyright. If it isn't copyrighted, you need to ask the editor to carry your copyright notice on your article when it is printed (otherwise your article will go into public domain). Also, if you plan to copyright your published articles as a group, a copyright notice must appear on each article when it is published, even if the magazine is copyrighted.

Q: Should a book be copyrighted in my name or the name of the publisher?

A: Under the new law, it should be copyrighted in the author's name, and most books are. However, there are still some publishers who prefer or even insist that it be copyrighted in the name of the company. This is negotiated in the book contract.

Q: What advantage is there in having a book copyrighted in the author's name, rather than the publisher's?

A: If it is in your name, the rights will automatically revert back to you when it goes out of print, and you are free to try to sell it to another publisher. If it is in the publisher's name, he can refuse to release it to you and can legally hold on to it for 35 years after publication, or 40 years after grant of copyright, whichever comes first.

Q: Who is responsible to put a copyright notice on my work before it is distributed?

A: The author is responsible. You must put the notice on your manuscript before sending it to a publisher.

there is no requirement that the phonore-cord bear a "C in a circle" notice to protect the underlying musical, dramatic, or literary work that is recorded.

Form of Notice for Phonorecords of Sound Recordings

The copyright notice for phonorecords of sound recordings (defined as "works that result from the fixation of a series of musical, spoken, or other sounds, but not including the sounds accompanying a motion picture or other audiovisual work, regardless of the nature of the material objects, such as disks, tapes, or other pho-norecords, in which they are embodied") has somewhat different requirements. The notice appearing on phonorecords should contain the following three elements:

1) The symbol ℗ (the letter P in a circle); and

2) The year of first publication of the sound recording; and

3) The name of the owner of copyright in the sound recording, or an abbreviation by which the name can be recognized, or a generally known alternative designation of the owner. If the producer of the sound recording is named on the phonorecord labels or containers, and if no other name appears in conjunction with the notice, the producer's name shall be considered a part of the notice.

"Is it okay to jazz up the copyright notice?"

℗ **1985 A.B.C., Inc.**
Note: Because of problems that might result in some cases from the variant forms of the notice, any form of the notice other than those given here should not be used without first seek-ing legal advice.

Position of Notice

The notice should be affixed to copies or phonorecords of the work in such a manner and location as to "give reasonable notice of the claim of copyright." The notice on phonorecords may appear on the surface of the phonorecord or on the phonorecord label or container, provided the manner of placement and location gives reasonable notice of the claim. The three elements of the notice should ordinarily appear together on the copies or phonorecords. The Copyright Office has issued regulations concerning the form and position of the copyright notice in the Code of Federal Regulations (37 C.F.R. Part 201); copies of these regulations are available from the Copyright Office as Circular R96 201.20.

The following locations and methods of affixation are acceptable; these examples are not exhaustive.

Works published in book form
1) Title page;
2) Page immediately following the title page;
3) Either side of the front or back cover;
4) First or last page of the main body of the work.

Single-leaf works
1) Front or back.

Works published as periodicals or other serials
1) Any location acceptable for books;
2) As part of or adjacent to the masthead or on the page containing the masthead;
3) Adjacent to a prominent heading, appearing at or near the front of the issue, containing the title of the periodical and any combination of the volume and issue

number and date of the issue.

Works published as separate contributions to collective works
For a separate contribution reproduced on only one page
    1) Under the title or elsewhere on the same page.
For a separate contribution reproduced on more than one page
    1) Under a title appearing at or near the beginning of the contribution;
    2) On the first page of the main body of the contribution;
    3) Immediately following the end of the contribution;
    4) On any of the pages where the contribution appears if the contribution consists of no more than 20 pages, the notice is reproduced prominently, and the application of the notice to the particular contribution is clear.

Works reproduced in machine-readable copies
    1) With or near the title or at the end of the work, on visually perceptible printouts;
    2) At the user's terminal at sign on;
    3) On continuous display on the terminal;
    4) Reproduced durably on a gummed or other label securely affixed to the copies or to a container used as a permanent receptacle for the copies.

Motion pictures and other audiovisual works
A notice embodied in the copies by a photomechanical or electronic process so that it ordinarily would appear whenever the work is performed in its entirety may be located:
    1) With or near the title;
    2) With the cast, credits, and similar information;
    3) At or immediately following the beginning of the work;
    4) At or immediately preceding the end of the work.

The notice on works lasting 60 seconds or less, such as untitled motion pictures or other audiovisual works, may be located:
    1) In all of the locations specified above for longer motion pictures; and,
    2) If the notice is embodied electronically or photomechanically, on the leader of the film or tape immediately preceding the work.

For audiovisual works or motion pictures distributed to the public for private use, the locations include the above, and in addition,
    1) On the permanent housing or container.

Pictorial, graphic, and sculptural works
For works embodied in two-dimensional copies, a notice should be affixed directly, durably, and permanently to:
    1) The front or back of the copies;
    2) Any backing, mounting, framing or other material to which the copies are durably attached, so as to withstand normal use.

For works reproduced in three-dimensional copies, a notice should be affixed directly, durably, and permanently to:
    1) Any visible portion of the work;
    2) Any base, mounting or framing or other material on which the copies are durably attached.

"What! No copyright notice?"

For works on which it is impractical to affix a notice to the copies directly or by means of a durable label, a notice is acceptable if it appears on a tag or durable label attached to the copy so that it will remain with it as it passes through commerce.

For works reproduced in copies or consisting of a sheet-like or strip material bearing multiple or continuous reproductions of the work, such as fabrics or wall paper, the notice may be applied:

1) To the reproduction itself;

2) To the margin, selvage, or reverse side of the material at frequent and regular intervals; or

3) If the material contains neither a selvage nor reverse side, to tags or labels attached to the copies and to any spools, reels, or containers housing them in such a way that the notice is visible in commerce.

Ommission of Notice and Error of Notice

The publication of copies or phonorecords with no notice or with an incorrect notice will not automatically invalidate the copyright or affect ownership. However, certain errors in the notice or publication without a notice, if not corrected, may eventually result in the loss of copyright protection or in a change in the length of the term of copyright protection. The extent of the remedies available to a copyright owner may also be affected when someone innocently infringes a copyright by relying on an authorized copy or phonorecord with no notice or with an incorrect notice.

Omission of Notice

"Omission of notice" is publishing without a notice. In addition, some errors are considered the same as omission of notice. These are:

1) A notice that does not contain the symbol © (the letter C in a circle), or the word "Copyright" or the abbreviation "Copr." or, if the work is a sound recording, the symbol ℗ (the letter P in a circle);

2) A notice dated more than one year later than the date of the first publication;

3) A notice without a name or date that could reasonably be considered part of the notice;

4) A notice that lacks the statement required for works consisting preponderantly of U.S. government material; and

5) A notice located so that it does not give reasonable notice of the claim of copyright.

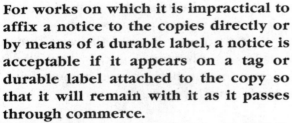

20

The omission of notice does not affect the copyright protection and no corrective steps are required if:

1) The notice is omitted from no more than a relatively small number of copies or phonorecords distributed to the public; or

2) The omission violated an express written requirement that the published copies or phonorecords bear the prescribed notice.

In all other cases of omission, to preserve copyright:

1) The work must have been registered before it was published in any form or before the omission occurred or it must be registered within five years after the date of publication without notice; and

2) The copyright owner must make a reasonable effort to add the notice to all copies or phonorecords that are distributed to the public in the United States after the omission is discovered.

If these corrective steps are not taken, the work will go into public domain in the United States five years after publication. At that time all U.S. copyright protection will be lost and cannot be restored.

Error in Year

Copyright protection under the current law generally lasts for the life of the author plus 50 years. However, in the case of anonymous and pseudonymous works and works made for hire, the copyright lasts for 75 years from the date of publication or 100 years from the year of creation, whichever expires first. If the copyright duration depends on the date of first publication and the year given in the notice is earlier than the actual publication date, the year in the notice could determine the length of protection. For a later date in the notice, see Omission of Notice.

Example: A work made for hire is created in 1980 and is first published in 1986. However, the notice contains the earlier year of 1985. In this case the term of copyright protection would be measured from the year in the notice and the expiration date would be 2060, 75 years from 1985.

Error in Name

When the person named in the notice is not the owner of copyright, the error may be corrected by:

1) Registering the work in the name of the true owner; or

2) Recording a document in the Copyright Office executed by the person named in the notice that shows the correct ownership.

"He says he didn't know it was copyrighted."

Otherwise, anyone who innocently infringes the copyright and can prove that he or she was misled by the notice and that the above steps were not taken before the infringement, will have a complete defense against the infringement.

Q: What if I quote material in my writing that appeared without a copyright notice, and I later find out the notice was left off in error. Am I liable?

A: The decision would be based on whether or not you would have reason to know there had been an error.

Q: What if I ask an editor to put a copyright notice on a piece when it is published and he doesn't? Or if he prints it incorrectly?

A: The copyright law does make provision to correct the omission of, or error in, a copyright notice if the proper steps are taken. A registration of the copyright notice must be made within five years after the publication without notice.

3 Reproductions of Copyrighted Works

You may use copies of copyrighted material when teaching

Q: How do you determine what constitutes fair use? Am I safe to assume that I can quote up to 250 words without getting permission?
A: When it comes to fair use, you can assume nothing. Although the law defines fair use (see below), it is not a black-and-white issue. Most questions fall into a gray area. The law gives no specific number of words that can safely be quoted without permission. You must read the limitations given below and make your own determination. Use your common sense. If the quote is of a minor nature, such as one anecdote from a whole book, you will probably not need to ask permission. However, if you take the 10 steps to a happy marriage, on which the book is based, you are taking the heart of that author's material, and would be infringing on his copyright. The only rule is: When in doubt, ask.

What is Fair Use?

The copyright law provides for "fair use" of another's work without infringing on his copyright. It is defined as the right to use copyrighted work without permission or making payment to the copyright owner.

The following is a reprint of the entire text of Section 107 of Title 17, *United States Code.*

§107. Limitations on exclusive rights: Fair use

Notwithstanding the provisions of Section 106, the fair use of a copyrighted work, including such use by reproduction in copies or phonorecords or by any other means specified by that section, for purposes such as criticism, comment, news reporting, teaching (including multiple copies for classroom use), scholarship, or research, is not an infringement of copyright. In determining whether the use made of a work in any particular case is a fair use the factors to be considered shall include—

(1) the purpose and character of the use, including whether such use is of a commercial nature or is for nonprofit educational purposes;

(2) the nature of the copyrighted work;

(3) the amount and substantiality of the portion used in relation to the copyrighted work as a whole; and

(4) the effect of the use upon the potential market for or value of the copyrighted work.

What About Permissions?

Whenever a writer questions if the amount of material he is quoting constitutes fair use, permission should be sought from the copyright owner. See Appendix C for a sample permission form.

Reproductions by Libraries and Archives

The copyright law provides that libraries and archives may make copies of copyrighted material under certain conditions. The following is a reprint of the entire text of Section 108 of Title 17, United States Code.

§108. Limitations on exclusive rights: Reproduction by libraries and archives

(a) Notwithstanding the provisions of Section 106, it is not an infringement of copyright for a library or archives, or any of its employees acting within the scope of their employment, to reproduce no more than one copy or phonorecord of a work, or to distribute such copy or phonorecord, under the conditions specified by this section, if—

(1) the reproduction or distribution is made without any purpose of direct or indirect commercial advantage; (2) the collections of the library or archives are (i) open to the public, or (ii) available not only to researchers affiliated with the library or archives or with the institution of which it is a part, but also to other persons doing research in a specialized field; and (3) the reproduction or distribution of the work includes a notice of copyright.

(b) The rights of reproduction and distribution under this section apply to a copy

Q: If I determine that I can quote from someone without getting permission, do I have to give them credit?

A: Yes, always give credit for quotes whether or not you have asked for permission to use them.

Q: Are there any types of material that I need to be especially careful about quoting from?

A: In most cases, you cannot quote from poetry or the words of a popular song without permission. You can only use the title. The exception would be old songs or hymns that are in public domain. Also, it is always necessary to obtain written permission for reprinting anything in its entirety, translating a work into another language, or using a piece in a collection or anthology.

Q: I do a lot of research at the library. Is it okay to make one photocopy of material I find that I want to take with me?

A: Yes, it's legal to do so.

Q: I teach writing classes regularly, and sometimes want to make copies of articles or other material from books or magazines to distribute to my students. I understand it's legal to make multiple copies like that as long as it's for nonprofit, educational purposes.

A: It depends. If you find something you would like to distribute to your students this week (or in the near future), it is acceptable to make multiple copies. However, if you are planning your curriculum for next term, and have time to obtain originals of the material for your students, it is not acceptable to make multiple copies, even for educational purposes. (See page **65 GUIDELINES***)*

Q: How do I go about asking for permission? I wouldn't usually have the author's address, so who do I ask? And how do I know if the author or the publisher holds the copyright?

A: In a book, the copyright notice will tell you whether it is copyrighted in the name of the author or publisher. In a periodical, you usually can't tell. In either case, you will contact the publisher first. He can tell you who holds the copyright, and if it's the author, can send you the address or forward your request directly.

Q: What information do I need when I ask for permission, and what exactly do I ask for?

A: You need to be specific about the portion of the work you plan to quote. You will give the title of

the book or article you want to quote from and exactly what lines of what pages you plan to quote. Indicate what credit line and copyright notice you intend to use, and ask for corrections if needed. Send two copies of the letter, so the author, after signing, can return one to you and keep the second for his files. A sample permission form may be found in Appendix C.

Q: Are permissions granted free, or is there a charge? If there is a charge, do I pay it or does the publisher?

A: Sometimes they are given free, other times you will be asked to pay. The amounts vary greatly (permissions to use song lyrics are generally high), and you are responsible to pay for them, not the publisher. If you are asked to pay, you must decide if the piece is worth the cost to you, or if you could use something else just as well.

Q: When do I ask for permissions—before I sell a book or article, or after?

A: Generally speaking, you do it after you sell a book (before it is published), but before you sell an article. However, if there are critical quotes in your book, you may want to do those first to be sure you can actually get the permissions you must have.

Q: Do I have to ask permission to use the contents of a letter someone has sent to me?

A: Yes. Although you you own the paper it is written on, the words belong to the person who wrote the letter, and you must get their permission to use it.

Q: What is plagiarism?

A: It is copying, using, or closely imitating someone else's material without permission, acknowledgement, or compensation, while representing it as your own work.

Q: Is plagiarism illegal?

A: Plagiarism is always unethical, but is only illegal if it infringes on someone else's copyright. You can plagiarize material that is in the public domain if you don't give the author credit, and present it as your own work. You will not be liable legally, but will soon earn a reputation for being unethical and untrustworthy.

"I'm glad the library loaned us these records!"

or phonorecord of an unpublished work duplicated in facsimile form solely for purposes of preservation and security or for deposit for research use in another library or archives of the type described by clause (2) of subsection (a), if the copy or phonorecord reproduced is currently in the collections of the library or archives.

(c) The right of reproduction under this section applies to a copy or phonorecord of a published work duplicated in facsimile form solely for the purpose of replacement of a copy or phonorecord that is damaged, deteriorating, lost, or stolen, if the library or archives has, after a reasonable effort, determined that an unused replacement cannot be obtained at a fair price.

(d) The rights of reproduction and distribution under this section apply to a copy, made from the collection of a library or archives where the user makes his or her request or from that of another library or archives, of no more than one article or other contribution to a copyrighted collection or periodical issue, or to a copy or phonorecord of a small part of any other copyrighted work, if—

(1) the copy or phonorecord becomes the property of the user and the library or archives has had no notice that the copy or phonorecord would be used for any purpose other than private study, scholarship, or research; and (2) the library or archives displays prominently, at the place where orders are accepted, and includes on its order form, a warning of copyright in accordance with requirements that the Register of Copy-

rights shall prescribe by regulation.

(e) The rights of reproduction and distribution under this section apply to the entire work, or to a substantial part of it, made from the collection of a library or archives where the user makes his or her request or from that of another library or archives, if the library or archives has first determined, on the basis of a reasonable investigation, that a copy or phonorecord of the copyrighted work cannot be obtained at a fair price, if—

(1) the copy or phonorecord becomes the property of the user, and the library or archives has had no notice that the copy or phonorecord would be used for any purpose other than private study, scholarship, or research; and (2) the library or archives displays prominently, at the place where orders are accepted, and includes on its order form, a warning of copyright in accordance with requirements that the Register of Copyrights shall prescribe by regulation.

(f) Nothing in this section—

(1) shall be construed to impose liability for copyright infringement upon a library or archivesor its employees for the unsupervised use of reproducing equipment located on its premises: Provided, That such equipment displays a noticethat the making of a copy may be subject to the copyright law;

(2) excuses a person who uses such reproducing equipment or who requests a copy or phonorecord under subsection (d) from liability for copyright infringement for any such act, or for any later use of such copy or phonorecord, if it exceeds fair use as provided by Section 107;

(3) shall be construed to limit the reproduction and distribution by lending of a limited number of copies and excerpts by a library or archives of an audiovisual news program, subject to clauses (1), (2), and (3) of subsection (a); or

(4) in any way affects the right of fair use as provided by section 107, or any contractual obligations assumed at any time by the library or archives when it obtained a copy or phonorecord of a work in its collections.

(g) The rights of reproduction and distribution under this section extend to the isolated and unrelated reproduction or distribution of a single copy or phonorecord of the same material on separate occasions, but do not extend to cases where the library or archives, or its employee—

(1) is aware or has substantial reason to believe that it is engaging in the related or concerted reproduction or distribution of multiple copies or phonorecords of the same material, whether made on one occasion or over a period of time, and whether intended for aggregate use by one or more individuals or for separate use by the individual members of a group; or

(2) engages in the systematic reproduction or distribution of single or multiple copies or phonorecords of material described in subsection (d): Provided, That nothing in this clause prevents a library or archives from participating in interlibrary arrangements that do not have, as their purpose or effect, that the library or archives receiving such copies or phonorecords for distribution does so in such aggregate quantities as to substitute for a subscription to or purchase of such work.

(h) The rights of reproduction and distribution under this section do not apply to a musical work, a pictorial, graphic or sculptural work, or a motion picture or other audiovisual work other than an audiovisual work dealing with news, except that no such limitation shall apply with respect to rights granted by subsections (b) and (c), or with respect to pictorial or graphic works published as illustrations, diagrams, or similar adjuncts to works of which copies are reproduced or distributed in accordance with subsections (d) and (e).

(i) Five years from the effective date of this Act, and at five- year intervals thereafter, the Register of Copyrights, after consulting with representatives of authors, book

"Maybe this wouldn't be 'fair use'!"

Q: What are reprints?
A: Reprints are copies of published material. Reprints should carry the copyright notice with the name of the magazine or book and the state that the material is reprinted by permission. Be sure to have written permission before you reprint.

Q: Can I make copies for personal use?
A: Yes, but copied copyrighted material may not be used for any other purpose legally, not even to distribute to friends or show to clients. This includes not only paper reprints, but audio and video reproductions as well.

Q: Are violations of the copyright warnings a serious offense?
A: Yes, and presumes an intent to violate the law. Jail may not be likely, but the fines can be very expensive.

Q: What is an infringement?
A: Each unauthorized use of copyrighted material.

Q: Is each infringement considered a separate violation?
A: Yes, and in lieu of actual damages the statues provide for damages of not less than $250 and up to $10,000; except where willfulness can be proven the court can increase damages to $50,000 per infringement.

and periodical publishers, and other owners of copyrighted materials, and with representatives of library users and librarians, shall submit to Congress a report setting forth the extent to which this section has achieved the intended statutory balancing of the rights of creators, and the needs of users. The report should also describe any problems that may have arisen, and present legislative or other recommendations, if warranted.

Copyright Office Regulations under Section 108

The following is the text of regulations adopted by the Copyright Office to implement Sections 108 (d) (2) and 108 (e) of the new copyright law (37 Code of Federal Regulations 201.14).

§ 201.14 Warnings of copyright for use by certain libraries and archives

(a) Definitions.

(1) "Display Warning of Copyright" is a notice under paragraphs (d) (2) and (e) (2) of Section 108 of Title 17 of the United States Code as amended by Pub. L. 94-553. As required by those sections the "Display Warning of Copyright" is to be displayed at the place where orders for copies or phonorecords are accepted by certain libraries and archives.

(2) An "Order Warning of Copyright" is a notice under paragraphs (d) (2) and (e) (2) of Section 108 of Title 17 of the United States Code a amended by Pub. L. 94-553. As required by those sections the "Order Warning of Copyright" is to be included on printed forms supplied by certain libraries and archives and used by their patrons for ordering copies or phonorecords.

(b) Contents. A Display Warning of Copyright and an Order Warning of Copyright shall consist of a verbatim reproduction of the following notice, printed in such size and form and displayed in such manner as to comply with paragraph (c) of this section:

NOTICE
WARNING CONCERNING
COPYRIGHT RESTRICTIONS

The copyright law of the United States (Title 17, *United States Code*) governs the making of photocopies or other reproductions of copyrighted material.

Under certain conditions specified in the law, libraries and archives are authorized to furnish a photocopy or other reproduction. One of these specified conditions is that the photocopy or reproduction is not to be "used for any purpose other than private study, scholarship, or research." If a user makes a request for, or later uses, a photocopy or reproduction for purposes in excess of "fair use," that user may be liable for copyright infringement.

This institution reserves the right to refuse to accept a copying order if, in its judgment, fulfillment of the order would involve violation of copyright law.

(c) Form and Manner of Use.

(1) A Display Warning of Copyright shall be printed on heavy paper or other durable material in type at least 18 points in size, and shall be displayed prominently, in such manner and location as to be clearly visible, legible, and comprehensible to a casual observer within the immediate vicinity of the place where orders are accepted.

(2) An Order Warning of Copyright shall be printed within a box located prominently on the order form itself, either on the front side of the form or immediately adjacent to the space calling for the name or signature of the person using the form. The notice shall be printed in type size no smaller than that used predominantly throughout the form, and in no case shall the type size be smaller than 8 points. The notice shall be printed in such manner as to be clearly legible, comprehensible, and readily apparent to a casual reader of the form.

Q: Can I use a small part of a popular song without receiving permission?
A: No, it can be very costly because songs are seldom allowed to be used without compensation— even for just a few notes!
Q: Can copyrighted computer programs be used for personal use on more than one computer?
A: Yes, if used for only personal use.
Q: What about business use of copyrighted programs on more than one computer?
A: You must purchase a separate program for each computer used for business purposes.
Q: Do you have to pay royalty rights to play a radio, T.V. or video in a public place?
A: Anytime you use a broadcast for the enjoyment of your customers or clients in which you charge for services, you must pay for broadcast rights.

NOTES:

4 Reproductions for the Blind and Physically Handicapped

One of the major programs of the Library of Congress is to provide Braille editions and special phonorecords of readings of works for the exclusive use of blind and physically handicapped individuals. This program is administered by the National Library Service for the Blind and Physically Handicapped (NLS).

What is the License?

The voluntary license under Section 710 of the Copyright Act gives permission and authorization to the Library of Congress "to reproduce the copyrighted work by means of Braille or similar tactile symbols, or by fixation of a reading in a phonorecord, or both, and to distribute the resulting copies or phonorecords solely for the use of the blind and physically handicapped."

These are a few examples of the many types of published works for which a license under Section 710 would be appropriate: novels, stories, general nonfiction, poetry, children's books, scholarly works, entire periodical issues, and some reference works.

How Can I Grant a Voluntary License?

Copyright owners are the only ones who may grant a voluntary license. Form TX, the appropriate application to use for copyright registration covering nondramatic literary works, contains a space for granting the license. See Form TX.

Obligations of the Library of Congress

If a license is granted under Section 710, the Library of Congress is required to:

1) identify the author and publisher of the work, and reproduce the copyright notice, as it appears on the copies of the books, on all copies and phonorecords and publisher of the work;

2) reproduce the work only by or on behalf of the Library of Congress;

3) reproduce the work only in the form of Braille (or other similar tactile symbols), or in the form of a fixation of a reading of the work in phonorecords (phonograph disks, cassettes, or open-reel magnetic tapes) specially designed for use of blind and physically handicapped individuals, or both, as designated by the copyright owner on the application form; and

4) distribute any reproductions made under the license by the Library of Congress solely for the use of blind and physically handicapped readers certified by competent authority as unable to read normal printed material as a result of physical limitations, under regulations prescribed by the Library of Congress for this service.

Note: Granting a license gives the Library of Congress permission to reproduce a work and distribute copies or phonorecords to blind and physically handicapped individuals, but it does not mean that the Library will do so. A number of factors, including the needs of handicapped readers, the availability of funds, and various technical considerations, must be weighed by the NLS in determining whether to include a work in the Library's program.

Length of License

Licenses go into effect on the effective date of registration for the work being licensed and, unless terminated, they last for the same duration as copyright in the work.

The copyright owner may terminate a license at any time by submitting to NLS a written statement of intent to terminate. Termination becomes effective 90 days after NLS receives the written statement, or at any later date set forth in the statement. Reproductions already made under the license before the effective date of termination may continue to be distributed and used after termination of the license. However, after the effective date of termination, the Library of Congress will be prohibited from reproducing any additional copies or phonorecords of the work without the consent of the copyright owner.

Further questions about the voluntary license may be answered directly by writing to NLS:

National Library Service for the Blind and Physically Handicapped (NLS)
Library of Congress
1291 Taylor Street NW
Washington, DC 20542

5   Investigation of a Work's Copyright Status

Agent Kit-Cat® Copyright Investigator.

Q: Why does a business need to know about copyright?

A: —The copyrights some companies hold are worth more than all of their other assets combined.

—The misuse of copyrights of others can be very costly.

—The copyright law is easy to use and does not require the use of an attorney.

Methods of Approaching a Copyright Investigation

There are several ways to investigate whether a work is under copyright protection and, if so, the facts of the copyright. These are the main ones:

• Examine a copy of the work (or, if the work is a sound recording, examine the disk, tape cartridge, or cassette in which the recorded sound is fixed, or the album cover, sleeve, or container in which the recording is sold) for such elements as a copyright notice, place and date of publication, author and publisher (see ''Notice of copyright'' in chapter one);

• Make a search of the Copyright Office catalogs and other records; or

• Have the Copyright Office make a search for you.

The records of the Copyright Office are open to inspection and searching by the public from 8:30 a.m. to 5:00 p.m. Monday through Friday (except legal holidays). The Copyright Office is located in the **Library of Congress, James Madison Memorial Building, 101 Independence Avenue SE, Washington, DC.**

30

Records freely available to the public include an extensive card catalog, an automated catalog containing records from 1978 forward, record books, and microfilm records of assignments and related documents. Other records, including correspondence files and deposit copies, are not open to the public for searching. However, they may be inspected upon request and payment of a $10 per hour search fee.

If you wish to do your own searching in the Copyright Office files open to the public, you will be given assistance in locating the records you need and in learning searching procedures. If the Copyright Office staff actually makes the search for you, a search fee must be charged.

"Let's see, now . . ."

Upon request, the Copyright Office will make a search of its records at the statutory rate of $10 for each hour or fraction of an hour consumed. Based on the information you furnish, the Copyright Office will provide an estimate of the total search fee. If you decide to have the Office staff conduct the search, you should send the estimated amount with your request. The Office will then proceed with the search and send you a typewritten report or, if you prefer, an oral report by telephone. If you request an oral report, please provide a telephone number where you can be reached during normal business hours (8:30-5:00).

Search reports can be certified on request, for an extra fee of $4. Certified searches are most frequently requested to meet the evidentiary requirements of litigation.

Your request, and any other correspondence, should be addressed to:

Reference and Bibliography Section, LM-451
Copyright Office
Library of Congress
Washington, DC 20559
(202) 287-6850

Note: The search fee does not include the cost of additional certificates, photocopies of deposits, or copies of other office records. For information concerning these services, request Circular R6 from the Copyright Office.

What Information Do I Need to Give?

The more detailed information you can furnish with your request, the less time-consuming and expensive the search will be. Please provide as much of the following information as possible:

- The title of the work, with any possible variants;
- The names of the authors, including possible pseudonyms;
- The name of the probable copyright owner, which may be the publisher or producer;
- The approximate year when the work was published or registered;
- The type of work involved (book, play, musical composition, sound recording, photograph, etc.);
- For a work originally published as a part of a periodical or collection, the title of that publication and any other information, such as the volume or issue number, to help identify it;
- Motion pictures are often based on other works such as books or serialized contributions to periodicals or other composite works. If you desire a search for an underlying work or for music from a motion picture, you must specifically request such a search. You must also identify the underlying works and music and furnish the specific titles, authors, and approximate dates of these works; and
- The registration number of any other copyright data.

Note: Unless your request specifies otherwise, Copyright Office searches include records pertaining to registrations, renewals, assignments and other recorded documents concerning copyright ownership. If you want the office to search any other special records such as notices of use, or if you want to exclude specific records from your search, please make this clear in your request.

Limitations on Searches

In determining whether or not to have a search made, you should keep the following points in mind:

No special lists
The Copyright Office does not maintain any listings of works by subject, or any lists of works that are in the public domain.

Contributions
Individual works, such as stories, poems, articles, or musical compositions that were published as contributions to a copyrighted periodical or collection, are usually not listed separately by title in Office records.

No comparisons
The Copyright Office does not search or compare copies of works to determine questions of possible infringement or to determine how much two or more versions of a work have in common.

Titles and names not copyrightable
Copyright does not protect names and titles, and our records list many different works identified by the same or similar titles. Some brand names, trade names, slogans, and phrases may be entitled to protection under the general rules of law relating to unfair competition, or to registration under the provisions of the trademark laws. Questions about the trademark laws should be addressed to the **Commissioner of Patents and Trademarks, Washington, DC 20231**. Possible protection of names and titles under common law principles of unfair competition is a question of state law.

No legal advice
The Copyright Office cannot express any opinion as to the legal significance or effect of the facts included in a search report.

"This is the last place to look . . ."

Searches are not always conclusive
Searches of the Copyright Office catalogs and records are useful in helping to determine the copyright status of a work, but they cannot be regarded as conclusive in all cases. The complete absence of any information about a work in the office records does not mean that the work is unprotected. The following are examples of cases in which information about a particular work may be incomplete or lacking entirely in the Copyright Office:

- Before 1978, unpublished works were entitled to protection at common law without the need of registration;
- Works published with notice prior to 1978 may be registered at any time within the first 28-year term; to obtain renewal protection, however, the claimant must register and renew such work by the end of the 28th year;
- For works that came under copyright protection after 1978, registration may be made at any time during the term of protection; it is not generally required as a condition of copyright protection;
- Since searches are ordinarily limited to registrations that have already been cataloged, a search report may not cover recent registration for which catalog records are not yet available;
- The information in the search request may not have been complete or specific enough to identify the work;

- The work may have been registered under a different title or as part of a larger work.

For further information about copyright searches, write the Copyright Office for Circulars R15, "Renewal of Copyright," R15a, "Duration of Copyright," R15t, "Extension of Copyright Terms," and R6, "Obtaining Copies of Copyright Office Records and Deposits."

Protection in Foreign Countries

"Where's Tuvalu?"

Even if you conclude that a work is in the public domain in the United States, this does not necessarily mean that you are free to use it in other countries. Every nation has its own laws governing the length and scope of copyright protection, and these are applicable to uses of the work within that nation's borders. Thus, the expiration or loss of copyright protection in the United States may still leave the work fully protected against unauthorized use in other countries. See chapter 6 for more information about copyright protection in other countries.

6 International Copyright Relations of the United States

International Copyright Protection

There is no such thing as an "international copyright" that will automatically protect an author's writings throughout the entire world. Protection against unauthorized use in a particular country depends, basically, on the national laws of that country. However, most countries do offer protection to foreign works under certain conditions, and these conditions have been greatly simplified by international copyright treaties and conventions.

The United States is a member of the Universal Copyright Convention (UCC), which came into force on September 16, 1955. Generally, a work by a national or domiciliary of a country that is a member of the UCC or a work first published in a UCC country may claim protection under the UCC. If the work bears the notice of copyright in the form and position specified by the UCC, this notice will satisfy and substitute for any other formalities a UCC member country would otherwise impose as a condition of copyright. A UCC notice should consist of the symbol © (C in a

Q: Will copyright protect my work throughout the world?

A: No. Copyright protection varies and depends on the agreements each country has signed. The United States has agreements with many countries; see the list below for reciprocal agreements.

34

circle) accompanied by the name of the copyright owner and the year of first publication of the work.

An author who wishes protection for his or her work in a particular country should first find out the extent of protection of foreign works in that country. If possible, this should be done before the work is published anywhere, since protection may often depend on the facts existing at the time of first publication.

If the country in which protection is sought is a party to one of the international copyright conventions, the work may generally be protected by complying with the conditions of the convention. Even if the work cannot be brought under an international convention, protection under the specific provisions of the country's national laws may still be possible. Some countries however, offer little or no copyright protection for foreign works.

The following list sets forth U.S. copyright relations of current interest with the other independent nations of the world. Each entry gives the country name and a statement of copyright relations as of October 1, 1985. The following code is used:

Bilateral Bilateral copyright relations with the United States by virtue of a proclamation or treaty, as of the date given. Where there is more than one proclamation or treaty, only the date of the first one is given.

BAC Party to the Buenos Aires Convention of 1910, as of the date given. U.S. ratification deposited with the Government of Argentina, May 1, 1911; proclaimed by the President of the United States, July 13, 1914.

None No copyright relations with the United States.

Phonogram Party to the Convention for the Protection of Producers of Phonograms Against Unauthorized Duplication of Their Phonograms, Geneva, 1971, as of the date given. The effective date for the United States was March 10, 1974.

SAT Party to the Convention Relating to the Distribution of Programme-Carrying Signals Transmitted by Satellite, Brussels, 1974, as of the date given. The effective date for the United States was March 7, 1985.

UCC Geneva Party to the Universal Copyright Convention, Geneva, 1952, as of the date given. The effective date for the United States was September 16, 1955.

UCC Paris Party to the Universal Copyright Convention as revised at Paris, 1971, as of the date given. The effective date for the United States was July 10, 1974.

Unclear Became independent since 1943. Has not established copyright relations with the United States, but may be honoring obligations incurred under former political status.

Afghanistan
None

Albania
None

Algeria
UCC Geneva August 28, 1973
UCC Paris July 10, 1974

Andorra
UCC Geneva September 16, 1955

Angola
Unclear

Antigua and Barbuda
Unclear

Argentina
Bilateral August 23, 1934
BAC April 19, 1950
UCC Geneva February 13, 1958
Phonogram June 30, 1973

Australia
  Bilateral March 15, 1918
  UCC Geneva May 1, 1969
  Phonogram June 22, 1974
  UCC Paris February 28, 1978

Austria
  Bilateral September 20, 1907
  UCC Geneva July 2, 1957
  SAT August 6, 1982
  UCC Paris August 14, 1982
  Phonogram August 21, 1982

Bahamas, The
  UCC Geneva December 27, 1976
  UCC Paris December 27, 1976

Bahrain
  None

Bangladesh
  UCC Geneva August 5, 1975
  UCC Paris August 5, 1955

Barbados
  UCC Geneva June 18, 1983
  UCC Paris June 18, 1983
  Phonogram July 29, 1983

Belau
  Unclear

Belgium
  Bilateral July 1, 1891
  UCC Geneva August 31, 1960

Belize
  UCC Geneva September 21, 1981

Benin (formerly Dahomey)
  Unclear

Bhutan
  None

Bolivia
  BAC May 15, 1914

Botswana
  Unclear

Brazil
  BAC August 31, 1915
  Bilateral April 2, 1957
  UCC Geneva January 13, 1960
  Phonogram November 28, 1975
  UCC Paris December 11, 1975

Brunei
  Unclear

Bulgaria
  UCC Geneva June 7, 1975
  UCC Paris June 7, 1975

Burkina Faso (formerly Upper Volta)
  Unclear

Burma
  Unclear

Burundi
  Unclear

Cambodia
  UCC Geneva September 16, 1955

Cameroon
  UCC Geneva May 1, 1973
  UCC Paris July 10, 1974

Canada
  Bilateral January 1, 1924
  UCC Geneva August 10, 1962

Cape Verde
  Unclear

Central African Republic
  Unclear

Chad
  Unclear

Chile
  Bilateral May 25, 1896
  BAC June 14, 1955
  UCC Geneva September 16, 1955
  Phonogram March 24, 1977

China
  Bilateral January 13, 1904

Colombia
  BAC December 23, 1936
  UCC Geneva June 18, 1976
  UCC Paris June 18, 1976

Comoros
  Unclear

Congo
  Unclear

Costa Rica[1]
  Bilateral October 19, 1899
  BAC November 30, 1916
  UCC Geneva September 16, 1955
  UCC Paris March 7, 1980
  Phonogram June 17, 1982

Cuba
  Bilateral November 17, 1903
  UCC Geneva June 18, 1957

Cyprus
  Unclear

Czechoslovakia
  Bilateral March 1, 1927
  UCC Geneva January 6, 1960
  UCC Paris April 17, 1980
  Phonogram January 15, 1985

Denmark
  Bilateral May 8, 1893
  UCC Geneva February 9, 1962
  Phonogram March 24, 1977
  UCC Paris July 11, 1979

Djibouti
  Unclear

Dominica
  Unclear

Dominican Republic[1]
  BAC October 31, 1912
  UCC Geneva May 8, 1983
  UCC Paris May 8, 1983

Ecuador
  BAC August 31, 1914
  UCC Geneva June 5, 1957
  Phonogram September 14, 1974

Egypt[2]
  Phonogram April 23, 1978

El Salvador
  Bilateral June 30, 1908 by virtue of Mexico
    City Convention, 1902
  Phonogram February 9, 1979
  UCC Geneva March 29, 1979
  UCC Paris March 29, 1979

Equatorial Guinea
  Unclear

Ethiopia
  None

Fiji
  UCC Geneva October 10, 1970
  Phonogram April 18, 1973

Finland
  Bilateral January 1, 1929
  UCC Geneva April 16, 1963
  Phonogram April 18, 1973

France
  Bilateral July 1, 1891
  UCC Geneva January 14, 1956
  Phonogram April 18, 1973
  UCC Paris July 10, 1974

Gabon
Unclear

Gambia, The
Unclear

Germany
Bilateral April 16, 1892

UCC Geneva with German Democratic Republic October 5, 1973
Phonogram with Federal Republic of Germany May 18, 1974

Germany July 10, 1974
SAT August 25, 1979
UCC Paris with German Democratic Republic December 10, 1980

Ghana
UCC Geneva August 22, 1962

Greece
Bilateral March 1, 1932
                  August 24, 1963

Grenada
Unclear

Guatemala[1]
BAC March 28, 1913
UCC Geneva October 28, 1964
Phonogram February 1, 1977

Guinea
UCC Geneva November 13, 1981
UCC Paris November 13, 1981

Guinea-Bissau
Unclear

Guyana
Unclear

Haiti
BAC November 27, 1919
UCC Geneva September 16, 1955

Holy See (See Vatican City)

Honduras[1]
BAC April 27, 1914

Hungary
Bilateral October 16, 1912
UCC Geneva January 23, 1971
UCC Paris July 10, 1974
Phonogram May 28, 1975

Iceland
UCC Geneva December 18, 1956

India
Bilateral August 15, 1947
UCC Geneva January 21, 1958
Phonogram February 12, 1975

Indonesia
Unclear

Iran
None

Iraq
None

Ireland
Bilateral October 1, 1929
UCC Geneva January 20, 1959

Israel
Bilateral May 15, 1948
UCC Geneva September 16, 1955
Phonogram May 1, 1978

Italy
 Bilateral October 31, 1892
 UCC Geneva January 24, 1957
 Phonogram March 24, 1977
 UCC Paris January 25, 1980
 SAT July 7, 1981

Ivory Coast
 Unclear

Jamaica
 None

Japan[3]
 UCC Geneva April 28, 1956
 UCC Paris October 21, 1977
 Phonogram October 14, 1978

Jordan
 Unclear

Kenya
 UCC Geneva September 7, 1966
 UCC Paris July 10, 1974
 Phonogram April 21, 1976
 SAT August 25, 1979

Kiribati
 Unclear

Korea
 Unclear

Kuwait
 Unclear

Laos
 UCC Geneva September 16, 1955

Lebanon
 UCC Geneva October 17, 1959

Lesotho
 Unclear

Liberia
 UCC Geneva July 27, 1956

Libya
 Unclear

Liechtenstein
 UCC Geneva January 22, 1959

Luxembourg
 Bilateral June 29, 1910
 UCC Geneva October 15, 1955
 Phonogram March 8, 1976

Madagascar (Malagasy Republic)
 Unclear

Malawi
 UCC Geneva October 26, 1965

Malaysia
 Unclear

Maldives
 Unclear

Mali
 Unclear

Malta
 UCC Geneva March 12, 1968

Mauritania
Unclear

Mauritius
UCC Geneva March 12, 1968

Mexico
Bilateral February 27, 1896
UCC Geneva May 12, 1957
BAC April 24, 1964
Phonogram December 21, 1973
UCC Paris October 31, 1975
SAT August 25, 1979

Monaco
Bilateral October 15, 1952
UCC Geneva September 16, 1955
Phonogram December 2, 1974
UCC Paris December 13, 1974

Mongolia
None

Morocco
UCC Geneva May 8, 1972
UCC Paris January 28, 1976
SAT June 30, 1983

Mozambique
Unclear

Nauru
Unclear

Nepal
None

Netherlands, The
Bilateral November 20, 1899
UCC Geneva June 22, 1967

New Zealand
Bilateral December 1, 1916
UCC Geneva September 11, 1964
Phonogram August 13, 1976

Nicaragua 1
BAC December 15, 1913
UCC Geneva August 16, 1961
SAT August 25, 1979

Niger
Unclear

Nigeria
UCC Geneva February 14, 1962

Norway
Bilateral July 1, 1905
UCC Geneva January 23, 1963
UCC Paris August 7, 1974
Phonogram August 1, 1978

Oman
None

Pakistan
UCC Geneva September 16, 1955

Panama
BAC November 25, 1913
UCC Geneva October 17, 1962
Phonogram June 29, 1974
UCC Paris September 3, 1980

Papua New Guinea
Unclear

Paraguay
BAC September 20, 1917
UCC Geneva March 11, 1962
Phonogram February 13, 1979

Peru
BAC April 30, 1920
UCC Geneva October 16, 1963
SAT August 7, 1985
Phonogram August 24, 1985

Philippines
Bilateral October 21, 1948 UCC status undetermined by UNESCO. (Copyright Office considers that UCC relations do not exist.)

Poland
Bilateral February 16, 1927
UCC Geneva March 9, 1977
UCC Paris March 9, 1977

Portugal
Bilateral July 20, 1893
UCC Geneva December 25, 1956
UCC Paris July 30, 1981

Qatar
None

Romania
Bilateral May 14, 1928

Rwanda
Unclear

Saint Christopher and Nevis
Unclear

Saint Lucia
Unclear

Saint Vincent and the Grenadines
Unclear

San Marino
None

Sao Tome and Principe
Unclear

Saudi Arabia
None

Senegal
UCC Geneva July 9, 1974
UCC Paris July 10, 1974

Seychelles
Unclear

Sierra Leone
None

Singapore
Unclear

Solomon Islands
Unclear

Somalia
Unclear

South Africa
Bilateral July 1, 1924

Soviet Union
UCC Geneva May 27, 1973

Spain
Bilateral July 10, 1895
UCC Geneva September 16, 1955
UCC Paris July 10, 1974
Phonogram August 24, 1974

Sri Lanka (formerly Ceylon)
UCC Geneva January 25, 1984
UCC Paris January 25, 1984

Sweden
  Bilateral June 1, 1911
  UCC Geneva July 1, 1961
  Phonogram April 18, 1973
  UCC Paris July 10, 1974

Switzerland
  Bilateral July 1, 1891
  UCC Geneva March 30, 1956

Syria
  Unclear

Tanzania
  Unclear

Thailand
  Bilateral September 1, 1921

Togo
  Unclear

Tongo
  Unclear

Trinidad and Tobago
  Unclear

Tunisia
  UCC Geneva June 19, 1969
  UCC Paris June 10, 1975

Turkey
  None

Tuvalu
  Unclear

Uganda
  Unclear

United Arab Emirates
  None

United Kingdom
  Bilateral July 1, 1891
  UCC Geneva September 27, 1957
  Phonogram April 18, 1973
  UCC Paris July 10, 1974

Upper Volta (See Burkina Faso)

Uruguay
  BAC December 17, 1919
  Phonogram January 18, 1983

Vanuatu
  Unclear

Vatican City (Holy See)
  UCC Geneva October 5, 1955
  Phonogram July 18, 1977
  UCC Paris May 6, 1980

Venezuela
  UCC Geneva September 30, 1966
  Phonogram November 18, 1982

Vietnam
  Unclear

Western Samoa
  Unclear

Yemen (Aden)
  Unclear

Yemen (San'a)
None

Yugoslavia
UCC Geneva May 11, 1966
UCC Paris July 10, 1974
SAT August 25, 1979

Zaire[4]
Phonogram November 29, 1977

Zambia
UCC Geneva June 1, 1965

Zimbabwe
Unclear

[1] This country became a party to the Mexico City Convention, 1902, effective June 30, 1908, to which the United States also became a party, effective on the same date. As regards copyright relations with the United States, this convention is considered to have been superseded by adherence of this country and the United States to the Buenos Aires Convention of 1910.
[2] For works other than sound recordings, none.
[3] Bilateral copyright relations between Japan and the United States, which were formulated effective May 10, 1906, are considered to have been abrogated and superseded by the adherence of Japan to the UCC Geneva, effective April 28, 1956.
[4] For works other than sound recordings, unclear.

Pending before the respective judiciary committees of the House of Representatives and Senate are bills aiming to bring the United States under an international law or treaty known as the 'Berne Convention', which dates back to 1886. Only provisions of the amendment specifically enacted would become law; the U.S. statute would remain as the basic law for this country—which, would remain superior to Berne.

7 Copyright Registration Procedures

"Too bad you didn't copyright it!"

Why Register a Work?

In general, copyright registration is a legal formality intended to make a public record of the basic facts of a particular copyright. However, except in two specific situations, registration is not a condition of copyright protection.

"Do I have to register the copyright?"

Q: How does the copyright law define "publication"?
A: *Publication is defined as distribution of copies of a work or sale (or other transfer) to the public. Offering to distribute copies (whether or not they actually sold) constitutes publication. A public performance does not.*

Under the present law, copyright is secured automatically when the work is created, and a work is "created" when it is fixed in a copy or phonorecord for the first time. In general, "copies" are are material objects from which a work can be read or visually perceived either directly or with the aid of a machine or device, such as books, manuscripts, sheet music, film, videotape, or microfilm. "Phonorecords" are material objects embodying fixations of sounds (excluding, by statutory definition, motion picture soundtracks), such as audio tapes and phonograph disks.

Example: a song (the "work") can be fixed in sheet music ('copies") or in phonograph disks ('phonorecords") or both.

If a work is prepared over a period of time, the part of the work existing in fixed form on a particular date constitutes the created work as of that date.

Works published with notice of copyright prior to January 1, 1978, must be registered and renewed during the first 28-year term of copyright to maintain protection.

Under sections 405 and 406 of the Copyright Act, copyright registration may be required to preserve a copyright that would otherwise be invalidated because the copyright notice was omitted from the published copies or phonorecords, or the name or year date was omitted, or certain errors were made in the year date.

Even though registration is not generally a requirement for protection, the copyright law provides several inducements or advantages to encourage copyright owners to make registration. Among these advantages are the following:

- Registration establishes a public record of the copyright claim;
- Registration is ordinarily necessary before any infringement suits may be filed in court;

"Boy, I'm glad I registered my copyright

within three months of publication."

Q: If a piece is copyrighted from the time I have it typed, why would I register a copyright?

A: Usually you won't unless you fear infringement. It is not usually necessary to register a copyright on short stories or articles of a general nature. The exception would be if your material is based on a great deal of specialized research or contains information or statistics not readily available to the public. Also, it must be registered if you plan to bring suit against an infringer, but the registration can be done anytime within five years of first publication, and the suit can be brought anytime within three years of the infringement. However, if you don't register your copyright until after the infringement (or less than three months after first publication), you can sue for actual damages and profits, but not for attorney's fees or statutory damages.

Q: How long do I have to register something?

A: A work can be registered anytime within the length of the copyright.

Q: Do I have to copyright a manuscript before I send it to an editor?

A: You don't have to register a copyright (fill out a form and send money to Washington, DC). Your manuscript has automatic copyright protection from the time it reaches a tangible form, including full protection of the law.

Q: Do I need to register the copyright on a book before I submit it?

A: Not unless it contains specialized information and you fear infringement. Usually all you need do is put the copyright notice on the manuscript as you would with an article.

Q: Are there any situations in which I am required to register a work before submitting it?

A: Yes. Before submitting a television, radio or movie script, your work needs to be registered with the Writers Guild of America. A copy of your script should be in unbound, standard 8 ½ x 11 inch format. Registration may be completed by mail. For more information write to the Writers Guild of America, West, Inc., 9855 Beverly Boulevard, Los Angeles, CA 90048, or call (213) 550-1000. Registration costs $10 for nonmembers, $5 for members, lasts for five years and is renewable.

- If made before or within five years of publication, registration will establish prima facie evidence in court of the validity of the copyright and of the facts stated in the certificate; and

- If registration is made within three months after publication of the work or prior to an infringement of the work, statutory damages and attorney's fees will be available to the copyright owner in court actions. Otherwise, only an award of actual damages and profits is available to the copyright owner.

Registration may be made at any time within the life of the copyright. Unlike the law before 1978, when a work has been registered in unpublished form, it is not necessary to make another registration when the work becomes published (although the copyright owner may register the published edition, if desired).

Publication and Registration

Publication is no longer the key to obtaining statutory copyright as it was under the Copyright Act of 1909. However, publication remains important to copyright owners.

The Copyright Act defines publication as follows:

'**Publication" is the distribution of copies or phonorecords of a work to the public by sale or other transfer of ownership, or by rental, lease, or lending. The offering to distribute copies or phonorecords to a group of persons for purposes of further distribution, public performance, or public display, constitutes publication. A public performance or display of a work does not of itself constitute publication.**

A further discussion of the definition of "publication" can be found in the legislative history of the Act. The legislative reports define "to the public" as distribution to persons under no explicit or implicit restrictions with respect to disclosure of the contents. The reports state that the definition makes it clear that the sale of phono-

records constitutes publication of the underlying work, for example, the musical, dramatic, or literary work embodied in a phonorecord. The reports also state that it is clear that any form of dissemination in which the material object does not change hands, for example, performances or displays on television, is not a publication no matter how many people are exposed to the work. However, when copies or phonorecords are offered for sale or release to a group of wholesalers, broadcasters, or motion picture theaters, publication does take place if the purpose is further distribution, public performance, or public display.

Publication is an important concept in the copyright law because upon publication, several significant consequences follow. Among these are:

- When a work is published, all published copies should bear a notice of copyright (see "Notice of Copyright" in chapter two);

- Works that are published with notice of copyright in the United States are subject to mandatory deposit with the Library of Congress (see the section on "Mandatory Deposits" later in this chapter);

- Publication of a work can affect the limitations on the exclusive rights of the copyright owner that are set forth in Sections 107 through 118 of the law;

- The year of publication is used in determining the duration of copyright protection for anonymous and pseudonymous works (when the author's identity is not revealed in the records of the Copyright Office) and for works made for hire;

- Deposit requirements for registration of published works differ from those for registration of unpublished works (see "How to Register a Work" later in this chapter).

Publication and Unpublished Collections

A work may be registered in unpublished form as a "collection," with one application and one fee, under the following con-

"Can I register my unpublished work, too?"

ditions:

1) The elements of the collection are assembled in an orderly form;

2) The combined elements bear a single title identifying the collection as a whole;

3) The copyright claimant in all the elements and in the collection as a whole is the same; and

4) All of the elements are by the same author, or, if they are by different authors, at least one of the authors has contributed copyrightable authorship to each element.

Note: Unpublished collections are indexed in the Catalog of Copyright Entries only under the collection titles.

Who May File an Application Form?

Copyright application forms may be sent in by the copyright owner. This could be:

1) **The author.** This is either the person who actually created the work, or, if the work was made for hire, the employer or other person for whom the work was prepared;

2) **The copyright claimant.** The copyright claimant is defined in Copyright Office regulations as either the author of the work or a person or organization that has obtained ownership of all the rights under the copyright initially belonging to the author. This category includes a person or organization who has obtained by contract the right to claim legal title to the copyright in an application for copyright registration;

*Q: **Do I have to wait until a piece is published before I can register the copyright?***
A: No, both unpublished and published material can be copyrighted.

*Q: **If I copyright something when it is unpublished, do I have to do it again once it is published?***
A: No, not unless you want to.

*Q: **What constitutes a collection?***
A: There are two main types of collections that can be copyrighted— published works or unpublished works. Every year you can put all your unpublished pieces into a binder of some type (loose-leaf, report cover), give them a title, such as ''The Unpublished Writings of John Doe, 1987,'' and register them under one $10 fee. You can do the same thing with all the pieces published during a 12-month period, provided a copyright notice in your name actually appeared on each piece when it was published, under one $10 fee.

*Q: **Why would I want to copyright seminars, programs or speeches?***
A: Besides preventing competitors from reproducing your valuable material, you may be able to license their use and reproduction for a profit.

*Q: **Are my creative advertisements copyrightable?***
A: Yes, and if you do not copyright them, they automatically go into the public domain, which means your costly artwork can be used by others for nothing.

*Q: **Should you copyright newspaper or magazine ads?***
A: Only if they contain original text or artwork (ie., poem, drawings, unique design, etc.).

"I'd like to register this, please."

3) The owner of exclusive right(s). Under the new law, any of the exclusive rights that go to make up a copyright and any subdivision of them can be transferred and owned separately, even though the transfer may be limited in time or place of effect. The term "copyright owner" with respect to any one of the exclusive rights contained in a copyright refers to the owner of that particular right. Any owner of an exclusive right may apply for registration of a claim in the work;

4) The duly authorized agent of such author, other copyright claimant, or owner of exclusive right(s). Any person authorized to act on behalf of the author, other copyright claimant, or owner of exclusive right(s) may apply for registration.

There is no requirement that applications be prepared or filed by an attorney.

Best Editions

The copyright law requires that copies or phonorecords deposited in the Copyright Office be of the "best edition" of the work. The law states that "The best edition of a work is the edition, published in the United States at any time before the date of deposit, that the Library of Congress determines to be most suitable for its purposes." For works first published only in a country other than the United States, the law requires the deposit of the best edition as first published.

When two or more editions of the same version of a work have been published, the one of the highest quality is generally considered to be the best edition. In judging quality, the Library of Congress will adhere to the criteria set forth below in all but exceptional circumstances.

Where differences between editions represent variations in copyrightable content, each edition is a separate version and "best edition" standards based on such differences do not apply. Each such version is a separate work for the purposes of the

The best edition is for the Copyright Office.

copyright law.

The criteria to be applied in determining the best edition of each of several types of material are listed below in descending order of importance. In deciding between two editions, a criterion-by-criterion comparison should be made. The edition which first fails to satisfy a criterion is to be considered of inferior quality and will not be an acceptable deposit.

Example: If a comparison is made between two hardbound editions of a book, one a trade edition printed on acid-free paper, and the other a specially bound edition printed on average paper, the former will be the best edition because the type of paper is a more important criterion than the binding.

I. Printed textual matter

A. Paper, Binding, and Packaging:

1. Archival-quality rather than less-permanent paper. 2. Hard cover rather than soft cover. 3. Library binding rather than commercial binding. 4. Trade edition rather than book club edition. 5. Sewn rather than glue-only binding. 6. Sewn or glued rather than stapled or spiral-bound. 7. Stapled rather than spiral-bound or plastic-bound. 8. Bound rather than loose-leaf, except when future loose-leaf insertions are to be issued. In the case of loose-leaf materials, this includes the submission of all binders and indexes when they are part of the unit as pub-

lished and offered for sale or distribution. Additionally, the regular and timely receipt of all appropriate loose-leaf updates, supplements, and releases including supplemental binders issued to handle these expanded versions, is part of the requirement to properly maintain these publications.   9. Slip-cased rather than nonslip-cased.

10. With protective folders rather than without (for broadsides).

11. Rolled rather than folded (for broadsides).

12. With protective coatings rather than without (except broadsides, which should not be coated).

B. Rarity:

   1. Special limited edition having the greatest number of special features.

   2. Other limited editions rather trade edition.

   3. Special binding rather than trade binding.

C. Illustrations:

   1. Illustrated rather than unillustrated.

   2. Illustrations in color rather than black and white.

D. Special Features:

   1. With thumb notches or index tabs rather than without.

   2. With aids to use such as overlays and magnifiers rather than without.

E. Size:

   1. Larger rather than smaller sizes. (Except that large-type editions for the partially-sighted are not required in place of editions employing type of more conventional size.)

II. Photographs

A. Size and finish, in descending order of preference:

   1. The most widely distributed edition.

   2. 8 x 10-inch glossy print.

   3. Other size or finish.

B. Unmounted rather than mounted.

C. Archival-quality rather than less-permanent paper stock or printing process.

Criteria for other works may be found in Circular R7b from the Copyright Office. Under regulations of the Copyright Office, potential depositors may request authorization to deposit copies or phonorecords of other than the best edition of a specific work (e.g., a microform rather than a printed edition of a serial), by requesting "special relief" from the deposit requirements. All requests for special relief should be in writing and should state the reason(s) why the applicant cannot send the required deposit and what the applicant wishes to submit instead of the required deposit.

Special Deposit Requirements

The Copyright Act gives the Register of Copyrights authority to issue regulations making adjustments in the statutory deposit requirements. These regulations as now issued require or permit, for particular classes, the deposit of identifying material instead of copies or phonorecords, the deposit of only one copy or phonorecord where two would normally be required, and in some cases material other than complete copies of the best edition.

For example, the regulations ordinarily require deposit of identifying material, such as photographs or drawings, when the work being registered has been reproduced in three-dimensional copies.

If you are unsure of the proper deposit required for your work, write to the Copyright Office and describe the work you wish to register.

Mandatory Deposits

Although a copyright registration is not required, the Copyright Act establishes a mandatory deposit requirement for works published with notice of copyright in the United States. In general, the owner of copyright, or the owner of the right of first publication in the work, has a legal obligation to deposit in the Copyright Office, within three months of publication in the United States, two copies (or, in the case of sound recordings, two phonorecords), for the use of the Library of Congress in national library programs. Failure to make the deposit can result in fines and other penalties, but does not affect copyright protection.

The law envisions that deposit will be made voluntarily to satisfy this requirement. To enforce this legal obligation, however, or to ensure a more rapid deposit of a work the Library needs promptly, the Register of Copyrights may make a written demand for the required deposit at any time after publication. If the required deposit is not made within three months of the demand, the person or organization obligated to make the deposit is liable for a fine of not more than $250 for each work plus the retail prie of the copies; if the refusal to comply is willful or repeated, an added fine of $2,500 may be incurred.

The Copyright Office has issued regulations exempting certain categories of works entirely from the mandatory deposit requirements, and reducing the obligation for certain other categories. These regulations also reduce the required number of copies or phonorecords from two to one for certain other categories.

Q: I published an article with a copyright notice, but it wasn't registered, and I received a request from the Copyright Office to send them two copies of it. Why is that? Do I have to send the copies?

A: The Copyright Office picks articles at random for submission to them. You are not required to register the copyright on them, but you are required to send the requested copies. If they are not sent within three months, you can be fined up to $250 for each article, plus the retail cost for them to purchase the articles. If you refuse to comply, the fine could be $2,500.

Q: Do I have to send the Library of Congress a copy of my book when it's published?

A: No, not unless you are self-publishing the book and it carries a copyright notice. Usually the publisher will take care of the Library of Congress mandatory deposits at the same time the copyright is being registered.

Use of Mandatory Deposits to Satisfy Registration Requirements

With respect to works published in the United States the Copyright Act contains a special provision under which a single deposit can be made to satisfy both the deposit requirements for the Library and the registration requirements. The provision requires that, in order to have this dual effect, the copies or phonorecords must be "accompanied by the prescribed application and fee" for registration.

For more information about mandatory deposit, contact the Copyright Office for Circular R7d; for information about exemptions see Part 202 of 37 Code of Federal Regulations, Chapter II, or write the Copyright Office.

Corrections and Amplifications of Existing Registrations

To deal with cases in which information in the basic registration later turns out to be incorrect or incomplete, the law provides for "the filing of an application for supplementary registration, to correct an error in copyright registration or to amplify the information given in a registration." The information in a supplementary registration augments but does not supersede that contained in the earlier registration. Note also that a supplementary registration is not a substitute for an original registration or for a renewal registration.

Form CA may be photocopied from the back of this book or may be obtained through the Copyright Office. For further information about supplementary registrations, write for Circular R8.

Application Forms

For Original Registration

Form TX: for published and unpublished non-dramatic literary works.

Form SE: for serials, works issued or intended to be issued in successive parts bearing numerical or chronological designations and intended to be continued indefinitely (periodicals, newspapers, magazines, newsletters, annuals, journals, etc.).

Form PA: for published and unpublished works of the performing arts (musical and dramatic works, pantomimes and choreographic works, motion pictures and other audiovisual works).

Form VA: for published and unpublished works of the visual arts (pictorial, graphic and sculptural works).

Form SR: for published and unpublished sound recordings.

For Renewal Registration

Form RE: for claims to renewal copyright in works copyrighted under the law in effect through December 31, 1977 (1909 Copyright Act).

For Corrections and Amplifications

Form CA: for supplementary registration to correct or amplify information given in the Copyright Office record of an earlier registration.

Other Forms for Special Purposes

Form IS: request for issuance of an Import Statement under the manufacturing provisions of the Copyright Act.

Form GR/CP: an adjunct application to be used for registration of a group of contributions to periodicals in addition to an application Form TX, PA, or VA.

Application forms may be photocopied from the back of this book, or obtained, free of charge, from the Copyright Office.

Q: Do I just write the Copyright Office and ask them to send the copyright registration form?

A: No, you must know which form to request. For most literary writing, ask for Form TX. If you want to register a collection, you must ask for Form TX plus Form GR/CP. A full list of forms follows. Each form contains full instructions for filling it out and submitting it.

Fees

The Copyright Act of 1976 (Title 17, *United States Code*), established statutory fees for services provided by the Copyright Office. These services include registering claims to copyright and renewal of claims, as well as recordation of documents, searches of copyright records, and other services.

All remittances should be sent in the form of a check, money order, or bank draft payable to: **Register of Copyrights.**

The Copyright Office cannot assume any responsiblity for the loss of currency sent in payment of copyright fees. If you are submitting material from outside the United States, please arrange for your remittances to be payable immediately in United States dollars. Your remittance may be in the form of an International Money Order or a draft on a United States bank. The Copyright Office cannot accept a check drawn on a foreign bank.

If a check received in payment of the registration fee is returned to the Copyright Office as uncollectible, the Copyright Office will take immediate steps to cancel the registration and will notify the remitter.

Q: How much does it cost to register a copyright?
A: Ten dollars for each piece, or a collection of pieces.

The fee for registration of an original, supplemental, or renewal claim is non-refundable, whether or not copyright registration is ultimately made.

Registration $10.00
(including supplementary registration)

Renewals . . . . $ 6.00
For the registration under section 304(a) of a claim to renewal of a subsisting copyright in its first term.

For a listing and explanation of other fees, write to the Copyright Office and request Circular R4.

"That will be $10, please."

Refund of Fees

Money remitted to the Copyright Office for original, basic, supplementary or renewal registration will not be refunded if the claim is rejected because the material deposited does not constitute copyrightable subject matter or because the claim is invalid for any reason. Payments made by mistake or in excess of the statutory fee will be refunded, but amounts of $5 or less will not be refunded unless specifically requested, and refunds of less than $1 may be made in postage stamps.

Deposit Accounts in the Copyright Office

The Copyright Office maintains a system of Deposit Accounts for the convenience of those who frequently use its services. The system allows an individual or firm to establish a Deposit Account in the Copyright Office and to make advance deposits into that Account. Deposit Account holders can charge copyright fees against the balance in their accounts instead of sending separate remittances with applications and other requests for services.

Deposit Accounts do not operate in the same way as commercial charge accounts, and cannot be overdrawn or used as a form of advance credit. Funds must be available in a Deposit Account for the payment of copyright fees before an application for registration can be accepted or other services performed.

Minimum Requirements for Deposit Accounts

- When the Account is opened, the initial deposit must amount to at least $250;
- All subsequent deposits into the Account must also be $250 or more;
- There must be at least 12 transactions a year;
- If fees are to be charged against a Deposit Account, the exact name and number of the Account must be given on all applications for registration or requests for services;
- The Deposit Account holder must maintain a sufficient balance to cover all charges against the Account. The Copyright Office will send holders monthly statements showing deposits, charges, and balances. However, for the reasons explained below, it is important for holders to keep their own records and to make sure that the Office is not forced to delay action because of insufficient funds in a Deposit Account.

Do not allow your Deposit Account to become depleted.

Effective December, 1982, the $10 copy-

right registration fee (and the $6 renewal claim fee) charged by the Copyright Office became nonrefundable fees charged for processing a copyright application; these fees are now retained for all applications, whether original, renewal, or supplementary, whether or not registration of copyright is ultimately made.

If there are insufficient funds in Accounts, Deposit Account holders may have to resubmit claims to copyright by sending another application and additional deposit copies of the work to be registered, as the first deposit copies may have already been transferred to other departments of the Library of Congress and no longer be available to the Copyright Office.

Also, sufficient funds are important because a copyright registration is effective on the date of receipt in the Copyright Office of all the required elements in acceptable form, including the fee.

If you wish to open a Deposit Account, write to:
Department DS Library of Congress Washington, DC 20540
Attention: Deposit Accounts
Please use this address only to open or replenish a Deposit Account. Do not use it to send materials for copyright registrations or to make inquiries about copyright.

How to Register a Work

Send the following three elements in the same envelope or package to the Copyright Office:
1) A properly completed application form;
2) A nonreturnable filing fee of $10 for each application; and
3) A nonreturnable deposit of the work being registered.

The deposit requirements vary in particular situations. The general requirements are:
• If the work is unpublished, one complete copy or phonorecord.
• If the work was first published in the United States on or after January 1, 1978, two complete copies or phonorecords of the best edition.
• If the work was first published in the United States before January 1, 1978, two complete copies or phonorecords of the work as first published.
• If the work was first published outside the United States, whenever published, one complete copy or phonorecord of the work as first published.
• If the work is a contribution to a collective work, and published after January 1, 1978, one complete copy or phonorecord of the best edition of the collective work.

Mailing the Registration Forms

The application, nonreturnable deposit (copies or phonorecords), and nonreturnable filing fee should be mailed in the same package or envelope to:
Register of Copyrights Copyright Office Library of Congress Washington, DC 20559

What Happens if the Three Elements Are not Received Together?

Applications and fees received without copies or phonorecords will not be processed and will ordinarily be returned. Unpublished deposits alone will ordinarily be returned, also. Published deposits received without applications and fees will be immediately transferred to the collections of the Library of Congress. This practice is in accordance with section 408 of the law which provides that the published deposit required for the collections of the Library of Congress may be used for registration only if the deposit is "accompanied by the prescribed application and fee..."

After the deposit is received and transferred to another department of the Library for its collections or other disposition, it is no longer available to the Copyright Office; the custody of that deposit has also been transferred to the other department. Then, if you wish to make copyright registration, you must deposit additional copies or phonorecords with your application and fee.

Effective Date of Registration

Please note that a copyright registration is effective on the date of receipt in the Copyright Office of all the required elements in acceptable form, regardless of the length of time it takes thereafter to process the application and mail the certificate of registration. The length of time required by the Copyright Office to process an application varies from time to time, depending on the amount of material received and the personnel available to handle it. It must also be kept in mind that it may take a number of days for mailed material to reach the Copyright Office and for the certificate of registration to reach the recipient after being mailed by the Copyright Office.

If you are filing an application for copyright registration in the Copyright Office, you will not receive an acknowledgement that your application has been received (the Office receives more than 500,000 applications annually), but you can expect:

Q: When does my copyright become effective?
A: Your copyright begins the day the Copyright Office receives all three elements required for a complete application—application form, nonreturnable deposit of the work and nonreturnable filing fee—even though you will not hear from the Copyright Office for up to 90 days. Many authors send their registration materials by certified or registered mail in order to have written notice of their receipt before that time.

You'll receive a notice in the mail

- A letter or telephone call from a copyright examiner if further information is needed;
- A certificate of registration to indicate the work has been registered, or if the application cannot be accepted, a letter explaining why it has been rejected.

You may not receive either of these until 90 days have passed.

If you want to know when the Copyright Office receives your material, you should send it via registered or certified mail and request a return receipt.

"If I had sent it by certified mail, I would know for sure."

Replying to Copyright Office Correspondence

In the event you do not reply to Copyright Office correspondence within 120 days:

1) The file on your case will be closed. You will not be notified when your file is closed;
2) Any published deposit you submitted will be made available to the Library of Congress for use or disposition under the

provisions of the copyright law, 17 U.S.C. § § 407, 704;

3) Any unpublished deposit you submitted will be returned to you;

4) Any copyright filing or renewal fee submitted with a deposit and application will not be refunded.

Consequences of a Closed File

If the Copyright Office closes the file and you later re-apply for registration:

1) You will be required to submit a new application, deposit, and fee; and

2) The effective date of registration will be based on the new, later submission.

NOTES:

Appendix A
Publications
on Copyright

Copyright Office Publications

The following is a list of publications (circulars and forms) that may be obtained, free of charge, from the Copyright Office. Order them by writing or calling:

Publications Section, LM-455
Copyright Office
Library of Congress
Washington, DC 20559

(202) 287-8700

Note: Requestors may order application forms or circulars at any time by telephoning (202) 287-9100. Orders will be recorded automatically and filled as quickly as possible.

"Next time I'll only ask for the form I need."

Application Forms

Form TX: For published and unpublished nondramatic literary works

Form SE: For registration of each individual issue of a serial

Form PA: For published and unpublished works of the performing arts (musical and dramatic works, pantomimes and choreographic works, motion pictures, and other audiovisual works)

Form VA: For published and unpublished works of the visual arts (pictorial, graphic, and sculptural works)

Form SR: For published and unpublished sound recordings

Form RE: For claims to renewal copyright in works copyrighted under the law in effect through December 31, 1977 (1909 Copyright Act)

Form CA: For supplementary registration to correct or amplify information given in the copyright record of an earlier registration

Form GR/CP: An adjunct application to be used for registration of a group of contributions to periodicals

Circulars

R1 Copyright Basics

R1b Limitations on the Information Furnished by the Copyright Office

R1c Copyright Registration Procedures

R1e The Certification Space of the Application Form

R2 Publications on Copyright

R2b Selected Bibliographies on Copyright

3 Copyright Notice

R4 Copyright Fees

R5 How to Open and Maintain a Deposit Account in the Copyright Office

R6 Obtaining Copies of Copyright Office Records and Deposits

R7b "Best Edition" of Published Copyrighted Works for the Collections of the Library of Congress

R7c The Effects of Not Replying Promptly to Copyright Office Correspondence

R7d Mandatory Deposit of Copies or Phonorecords for the Library of Congress

R8 Supplementary Copyright Registration

R9 Works-Made-For-Hire Under the 1976 Copyright Act

RSL9 General Announcement

RSL9a Separate Application Forms and Continuation Sheets

R12 Recordation of Transfers and Other Documents

R13 Trademarks

R15 Renewal of Copyright

R15a Duration of Copyright

R15t Extension of Copyright Terms

R21 Reproduction of Copyrighted Works by Educators and Librarians

R22 How to Investigate the Copyright Status of a Work

R23 The Copyright Card Catalog and the Online Files of the Copyright Office

R30 Special Postage Rates for Deposit Copies Mailed to the Copyright Office

R31 Ideas, Methods, or Systems

R32 Blank Forms and Other Works Not Protected by Copyright

33 Computing and Measuring Devices

R34 Copyright Protection Not Available for Names, Titles, or Short Phrases

R38a International Copyright Relations of the United States

R40a Specifications for Visual Arts Identifying Material

R40b Deposit Requirements for Registration of Claims to Copyright in Visual Arts Material

R44 Cartoons and Comic Strips

R45 Copyright Registration for Motion Pictures Including Video Recordings

47e Radio and Television Programs

R49 Registration for Video Games and Other Machine-readable Audiovisual Works

R50 Copyright Registration for Musical Compositions

R51 Repeal of Notice of Use Requirement

R56 Copyright for Sound Recordings

R56a Copyright Registration of Musical Compositions and Sound Recordings

R61 Copyright Registration for Computer Programs

R62 Copyright Registration for Serials on Form SE

NOTES:

Appendix B
Bibliographies on Copyright

"Could you show me what you have on copyright?"

Bibliography on Copyright

This bibliography contains reference material relevant both to copyright issues under the Copyright Act of 1976 (the general revision of the copyright law which became effective January 1, 1978), and to the previous 1909 statute, which the revision supersedes. The copyright statute is found in title 17 of the United States Code.

The list of works is not intended to be exhaustive, nor does the Copyright Office necessarily endorse the works listed. Year dates of publications have not been given for works revised annually or at frequent intervals.

United States

American Law Institute-American Bar Association. *The Copyright Act of 1976*. Philadelphia: American Law Institute-American Bar Association, 1976.

Brunnin, Brad and Beren, Peter. *Author Law and Strategies: A Legal Guide for the Working Writer*. Berkeley: Nolo Press, 1983.

Bush, George P. *Technology and Copyright: Sources and Materials*. Mt. Airy, Maryland: Lomond Books, 1979.

Chickering, Robert B., and Susan Hartman. *How to Register a Copyright and Protect Your Creative Work*. New York: Charles Scribner's Sons, 1980.

Commerce Clearing House. *Copyright Law Reporter*. Chicago: Commerce Clearing House, 1980 (2 v. loose-leaf).

Copyright Law Symposium. *Nathan Burkan Memorial Competition*, sponsored by the American Society of Composers, Authors, and Publishers. New York: Columbia University Press, 1939-. (The essays contained in each volume are selected annually for inclusion.)

Copyright Society of the U.S.A. *Bulletin*. New York: New York University Law Center, 1953-. (Published bimonthly.)

Copyright Society of the U.S.A. *Studies on Copyright*. Compiled and edited under the supervision of the Copyright Society of the U.S.A. 2 v. Arthur Fisher Memorial Edition. South Hackensack, New Jersey: F.B. Rothman, and Indianapolis: Bobbs-Merrill Co., 1963.

Crawford, Tad. *The Writer's Legal Guide*. New York: Hawthorn Books, Inc, 1977.

Gaston, Janice B. *The New Copyright Law: A Handbook for Noncommercial Broadcasters*. Washington, DC: National Public Radio, 1978 (loose-leaf).

Heller, James S. and Wiant, Sarah K. *Copyright Handbook*. Littleton, Colorado: Fred B. Rothman & Co., 1984.

Henn, Harry G. *Copyright Primer*. New York: Practising Law Institute, 1979.

Hirsch, E.G. *Copyright It Yourself*. Wheeling, Illinois: Whitehall, Co., 1979.

Hurst, Walter E. *Copyright: How to Register Your Copyright and Introduction to New and Historial Copyright Law*. Hollywood: Seven Arts Press, 1977.

Hurst, Walter E. *Copyright Registration Forms PA and SR: How to Prepare Applications to Register Songs, Movies, Performing Arts Works and Sound Recordings With the U.S. Copyright Office*. 1st ed. Hollywood: Seven Arts Press, 1978.

Johnston, Donald F. *Copyright Handbook*. New York: R.R. Bowker Co., 1978.

Kaplan, Benjamin, and Ralph S. Brown, Jr. *Cases on Copyright, Unfair Competition, and Other Topics Bearing on the Protection of Literary, Musical, and Artistic Works*. 3d ed. by Ralph S. Brown, Jr. Mineola, New York: Foundation Press, 1978.

Kozak, Ellen M. *Every Writer's Practical Guide to Copyright: Fifty Questions and Answers*. St. Paul: Inkling Publications, 1985.

Latman, Alan. *The Copyright Law: Howell's Copyright Law Revised and the 1976 Act*. 5th ed. Washington, DC: Bureau of National Affairs, 1979.

Latman, Alan, and Ralph Gorman. *Copyright for the Eighties. Cases and Materials*. Charlottesville, Virginia: Michie Bobbs-Merrill, 1981.

Lawrence, John S. and Timbey, Bernard, eds. *Fair Use and Free Inquiry: Copyright Law and the New Media*. Norwood, New Jersey: Ablex Publications, 1980.

Lindey, Alexander. *Lindey on Entertainment, Publishing and Arts; Agreements and the Law*. New York: Clark Boardman, 1980- (loose-leaf).

Medical Library Association. *The Copyright Law and the Health Sciences Librarian*. Chicago: Medical Library Association, 1978.

Nimmer, Melville B. *Cases and Materials on Copyright and Other Aspects of Law Pertaining to Literary, Musical and Artistic Works*. 2d ed. (American Casebook Series). St. Paul: West Publishing Co., 1979.

Nimmer, Melville B. *Nimmer on Copyright*. Albany, New York: M. Bender, 1982 (4 v. loose-leaf).

Patent, Trademark and Copyright Journal. Washington, DC: Bureau of National Affairs, 1970-. (Beginning with November 5, 1970, published every Thursday except the Thursday following July 4 and the last Thursday in December.)

Patterson, Lyman Ray. *Copyright in Historical Perspective*. Nashville: Vanderbilt University Press, 1968.

Patton, Warren L. *An Author's Guide to the Copyright Law*. Lexington, Massachusetts: Lexington Books, 1980.

Ringer, Barbara. *The demonology of copyright*. New York: R.R. Bowker Co., 1974.

Rosenberg, Peter D. *Patent Law Fundamentals*. New York: Clark Boardman, 1980.

Seidel, Arthur H. *What the General Practitioner Should Know About Trademarks, and Copyright*. 4th ed. Philadelphia: American Law Institute, 1979.

Shemel, Sidney, and M. William Krasilovsky. *This Business of Music*. Ed. by Paul Ackerman. Rev. and enl. 4th ed. New York: Billboard Publications, Inc., 1979.

Sparkman, Joseph B. *Copyright Primer for Film and Video*. Portland, Oregon: Northwest Media Project, 1978.

Strong, William S. *The Copyright Book: A Practical Guide*. 2nd ed. Cambridge, Massachusetts: MIT Press, 1984.

Stuart, Sally E. and Woody Young. *Copyright Not Copycat: A Writer's Guide to Copyright*. *San Juan Capistrano, Ca: Joy Publishing, 1987*.

Tucciarone, Angel. *Copyright and the Church Musician*. Pittsburgh: Diocese of Pittsburgh, 1977.

Unesco. *The ABC of Copyright*. Lanham, Maryland: Unipub, 1981.

United States, National Commission on New Technological Uses of Copyrighted Works (CONTU). *Final Report of CONTU on New Technological Uses of Copyrighted Works*. Washington, DC: Library of Congress, 1979.

Wincor, Richard. *Copyright, Patents, and Trademarks: The Protection of Intellectual and Industrial Property*. Dobbs Ferry, New York: Oceana Publications, 1980.

Wittenberg, Philip. *The Protection of Literary Property*. Boston: The Writer, Inc., 1978.

British and Canadian

Copinger, Walter Arthur. *Copinger and Skone James on the Law of Copyright*. 12th ed., by E. P. Skone James. London: Sweet & Maxwell, 1980.

Fox, Harold G. *The Canadian Law of Copyright and Industrial Designs*. 2d ed. Toronto: Carswell Co., 1967.

Keyes, A.A. *Copyright in Canada: Proposals for a Revision of the Law*. Hull, Quebec: Consumer and Corporate Affairs Canada, 1977.

International

Bogsch, Arpad L. *The Law of Copyrights Under the Universal Convention*. 3d rev. ed. Leyden: A. W. Sijhoff; New York: R.R. Bowker, 1968.

Copyright; Monthly Review of the World Intellectual Property Organization (WIPO). Geneva: WIPO, 1965-.

Copyright Laws and Treaties of the World. Compiled by the United Nations Educational, Scientific, and Cultural Organization with the cooperation of the Copyright Office of the United States of America and the Industrial Property Department of the Board of Trade of the United Kingdom of Great Britain and Northern Ireland. Edited by Arpad L. Bogsch, Harold W. Clarke, Juan O. Diaz-Lewis, Abe A. Goldman, and Thomas Ilosvay. 3 v. Paris: UNESCO; Washington, DC: Bureau of National Affairs, 1956- (loose-leaf). Kept up-to-date by annual supplements, 1957-.

Newcity, Michael A. *Copyright Law in the Soviet Union*. New York: Praeger, 1978.

Russell-Clarke, Alan Daubeny. *Russell-Clarke on Copyright in Industrial Designs*. 5th ed. London: Sweet & Maxwell, 1974.

Thomas, Denis. *Copyright and the Creative Artist: The Protection of Intellectual Property with Special Reference to Music*. London: Institute of Economic Affairs, 1967.

United Nations Educational, Scientific and Cultural Organization. Copyright Division. *Copyright Bulletin*. Paris, 1967-. (Published quarterly.)

Universal Copyright Convention Analyzed. Ed. by Theodore R. Kupferman and Mathew Foner. New York: Federal Legal Publications, 1955.

Selected Bibliography for Writers

Audiovisual Market Place. New York: R.R. Bowker Co.

Guide to Book-Publishing. New York: R.R. Bowker Co.

International Literary Market Place. New York: R.R. Bowker Co.

International Motion Picture Almanac. New York: Quigley Publishing Co., Inc.

International Television Almanac. New York: Quigley Publishing Co., Inc.

LMP (Literary Market Place). New York: R.R. Bowker Co.

Literary & Library Prizes. New York: R.R. Bowker Co.

The Writer. Boston: The Writer, Inc. (Published monthly.)

Writers' & Artists' Yearbook. Boston: The Writer, Inc.

Writer's Digest. Cincinnati: Writer's Digest, Inc. (Published monthly.)

Writer's Handbook. Boston: The Writer, Inc.

Writer's Market. Cincinnati: Writer's Digest, Inc.

Writer's Yearbook. Cincinnati: Writer's Digest, Inc.

Selected Bibliography for Artists

American Artist. New York: Billboard Publications, Inc. (Published monthly.)

Art in America. New York: Art in America. (Published bimonthly.)

Artist's Market. Cincinnati: Writer's Digest, Inc.

ARTnews. New York: ARTnews Associates. (Published ten times a year.)

Chamberlain, Betty. *The Artist's Guide to His Market*. Cincinnati: Watson: Guptill Publications.

Fine Arts Market Place. New York: R.R. Bowker Co.

Selected Bibliography for Musicians

Billboard. New York: Billboard Publications, Inc. (Published weekly.)

Dachs, David. *Anything Goes: The World of Popular Music*. Indianapolis: The Bobbs-Merrill Co., Inc.

Erickson, J. Gunnar; Hearn, Edward R., and Halloran, Mark E. *Musician's Guide to Copyright*. New York: Charles Scribner's Sons, 1983.

The Musician's Guide. New York: Music Information Service, Inc.

Pavlakis, Christopher. *The American Music Handbook*. New York: The Free Press.

Rachlin, Harvey. *The Encyclopedia of the Music Business*. New York: Harper and Row, 1981.

Shemel, Sidney, and M. Wiliam Krasilovsky. *More About This Business of Music*. New York: Billboard Publications, Inc., 1982.

Shemel, Sidney, and M. William Krasilovsky. *This Business of Music*. New York: Billboard Publications, 1979.

Variety. New York: Variety, Inc. (Published weekly.)

Selected Agencies and Associations for Song Writers and Musicians

The Harry Fox Agency, Inc., National Music Publishers Assoc., 205 E. 42nd Street, New York, New York 10017.

Music Publishers Association of the United States, 130 W. 57th Street, New York, New York 10019.

Production Music Library Association, 40 E. 49th Street, Suite 605, New York, New York 10017.

Appendix C
PERMISSION FORM

Dear Sir/Madam:

I am preparing a book/article titled _____ which will be
published by _____. It is scheduled to be released
_____.

Attached is a quote I would like to use. The material was taken from pages _____ of
_____ by _____.
The following is the credit line I will use. Please check it for accuracy and make any changes
that are necessary.

© 1987 John Doe

I would like permission to use this quote in my book/article and in all future revisions and editions thereof, including nonexclusive world rights in all languages. These rights will in no way restrict republication of the material by you or those you authorize.

Please sign this form in the appropriate places and return one copy to me in the enclosed stamped envelope. The second copy is for your files.

Should you not control these rights, please let me know the name and address of the person I should contact.

I appreciate your granting this request.

Sincerely,

Your Name _____

I (We) grant permission for use(s) requested above.

_____   _____

_____

Date _____

Guidelines: Not-For-Profit Classroom Use

I. *Single Copying for Teachers*

A single copy may be made of any of the following by or for a teacher at his or her individual request for his or her scholarly research or use in teaching or preparation to teach a class:

A. A chapter from a book;

B. An article from a periodical or newspaper;

C. A short story, short essay or short poem, whether or not from a collective work;

D. A chart, graph, diagram, drawing, cartoon or picture from a book, periodical, or newspaper.

II. *Multiple Copies for Classroom Use*

Multiple copies (not to exceed in any event more than one copy per pupil in a course) may be made by or for the teacher giving the course for classroom use or discussion; provided that:

A. The copying meets the tests of brevity and spontaneity as defined below; and,

B. Meets the cumulative effect test as defined below; and,

C. Each copy includes a notice of copyright.

Definitions

Brevity

(i) Poetry: (a) A complete poem if less than 250 words and if printed on not more than two pages or, (b) from a longer poem, an excerpt of not more than 250 words.

(ii) Prose: (a) Either a complete article, story or essay of less than 2,500 words, or (b) an excerpt from any prose work of not more than 1,000 words or 10% of the work, whichever is less, but in any event a minimum of 500 words.

[Each of the numerical limits stated in "i" and "ii" above may be expanded to permit the completion of an unfinished line of a poem or of an unfinished prose paragraph.]

(iii) Illustration: One chart, graph, diagram, drawing, cartoon or picture per book or per periodical issue.

(iv) "Special" works: Certain works in poetry, prose or in "poetic prose" which often combine language with illustrations and which are intended sometimes for children and at other times for a more general audience fall short of 2,500 words in their entirety. Paragraph "ii" above notwithstanding such "special works" may not be reproduced in their entirety; however, an excerpt comprising not more than two of the published pages of such special work and containing not more than 10% of the words found in the text thereof, may be reproduced.

Spontaneity

(i) The copying is at the instance and inspiration of the individual teacher, and

(ii) Not more than one short poem, article, story, essay or two excerpts may be copied from the same author, nor more than three from the same collective work or periodical volume during one class term.

Cumulative Effect

(i) The copying of the material is for only one course in the school in which the copies are made.

(ii) Not more than one short poem, article, story, essay or two excerpts may be copied from the same author, nor more than three from the same collective work or periodical volume during one class term.

(iii) There shall not be more than nine instances of such multiple copying for one course during one class term.

[The limitations stated in "ii" and "iii" above shall not apply to current news periodicals and newspapers and current news sections of other periodicals.]

III. *Prohibitions as to I and II Above*

Not withstanding any of the above, the following shall be prohibited:

(A) Copying shall not be used to create or to replace or substitute for anthologies, compilations or collective works. Such replacement or substitution may occur whether copies of various works or excerpts therefrom are accumulated or reproduced and used separately.

(B) There shall be no copying of or from works intended to be "consumable" in the course of study or of teaching. These include workbooks, exercises, standardized tests and test booklets and answer sheets and like consumable material.

(C) Copying shall not:

(a) substitute for the purchase of books, publishers' reprints or periodicals;

(b) be directed by higher authority;

(c) be repeated with respect to the same item by the same teacher from term to term.

(d) No charge shall be made to the student beyond the actual cost of the photocopying.

Appendix D
Glossary of Terms

"Now, what is the right word to use?"

Author *Creator of original, intellectual work such as books, computer programs, photographs, or sculpture.*

Best Edition *Copy of highest quality of a book or shorter work which is sent to Copyright Office when registering a copyright.*

Collection *A series of works that are gathered together (for example, anthologies) for publication or copyright registration purposes. May be published or unpublished for copyright registration.*

Copyright *Protection given to authors of original works including literary, dramatic, musical, artistic and other intellectual works. Copyright protection is available to published and unpublished works.*

Co-author *Person who participates with another in the creation of a work. This will affect ownership and length of copyright.*

Deposit Account *Account in which those who register copyrights may keep an amount of money available for use by the Copyright Office in registering copyrights.*

Derivative Works *All works that stem from one original creation, i.e., a movie, based on a book, is considered a derivative work.*

Fair Use *A provision of the copyright law that permits the use of a short portion of copyrighted material without getting permission from or infringing on the rights of the copyright owner.*

Free-lance Writer *Author who sells works on an individual basis to various publishers. Is not considered to be an employee of a publisher. (See "Work for Hire" definition below.)*

Infringement *Violation of another person's copyright ownership, by using copyrighted material without permission to an extent that does not constitute fair use.*

Manuscript *Work in tangible form, either on paper or computer diskette, that is offered for sale to a publisher.*

Name *That by which a product, company, etc. is known to the public. Cannot usually be copyrighted, but can be trademarked.*

Periodical *Magazine or newspaper. Authors sell "serial" rights to periodicals.*

Plagiarism *To copy, use or closely imitate another author's work, without compensation or permission, and represent it as your own.*

Public Domain *Term used to describe works no longer under copyright protection; copyright has either expired or notice of copyright never appeared on work. Works in public domain may not be copyrighted but a rewritten version may be copyrighted.*

Publication *Distribution, or offering to distribute, copies of a work or sale (or other transfer) to the public. A public performance of a dramatic work does not constitute publication.*

Publisher *Individual or company that produces copies of author's work.*

Registration *Securing a public record of copyright ownership. May be done before or after publication. Registration establishes prima facie evidence in case of infringement.*

Rights

All Rights *Publisher gets complete rights; author forfeits all rights to further use. Buyer can use however and as often as he wants without making further payment. Advisable only if price is right. If you sell all rights, they revert back to you after 35 years, unless you sign a work-for-hire contract.*

Exclusive Rights *Term used interchangeably with all rights.*

First Rights *Right to use a piece of writing for the first time. After work is printed, you may resell it. First rights usually implies one-time use, but it is best to state that in writing.*

One-time Rights *Right to publish one time. Writer can resell, outside of publication area, after it has been published. Usually applies to photo or graphic material, but also writing, especially in newspapers.*

Reprint Rights *Right to reprint work that originally appeared in another publication. First Reprint Rights indicates you are offering second use. The term Second Rights is used interchangeably with Reprint Rights.*

Serial Rights *Right to use a piece in a periodical (serial). Used in combination with other rights:*

First Serial Rights *First use in periodical. You still own first book rights and second serial rights (reprint rights).*

First North American Serial Rights *First use in periodical in North America. You still have right to sell in Europe, etc.*

Simultaneous Rights *Selling right to print a piece simultaneously to more than one buyer. Usually nonoverlapping markets. Never sell simultaneous rights unless all parties involved know you are doing so.*

Subsidiary Rights *Rights to a book, other than book publication, including paperback, book club, dramatic, radio, television, movie, foreign language translation, foreign reprint, audiovisual production, novelty and serial rights which may be negotiated on an individual basis.*

Serial *Term used to describe sales to periodicals (newspapers and magazines), not to be confused with serialization, the sale of a book to appear in consecutive issues of a periodical.*

Slogan *Phrase by which a company or product is known. Cannot usually be copyrighted but may be trademarked.*

Statutory Damages *Legal term used when copyright owner brings suit against an infringer because law (statute) has been broken. As with attorney's fees, statutory damages may be awarded to owner only if the copyright was registered within three months after publication of the work.*

Tangible Form *Work that is in a fixed form, i.e., on paper or computer diskette, if it is a book. At this point the work is copyrighted even if it hasn't been registered with the Copyright Office.*

Title *Name of book, article, etc. Cannot usually be copyrighted but may be trademarked.*

Unpublished *Works that have not been distributed to the public.*

Work for Hire *Contract drawn up between author and publisher stating that author is hired to do a specific writing job and publisher owns all rights to it.*

Filling Out Application Form TX

Detach and read these instructions before completing this form. Make sure all applicable spaces have been filled in before you return this form.

BASIC INFORMATION

When to Use This Form: Use Form TX for registration of published or unpublished non-dramatic literary works, excluding periodicals or serial issues. This class includes a wide variety of works: fiction, non-fiction, poetry, textbooks, reference works, directories, catalogs, advertising copy, compilations of information, and computer programs. For periodicals and serials, use Form SE.

Deposit to Accompany Application: An application for copyright registration must be accompanied by a deposit consisting of copies or phonorecords representing the entire work for which registration is to be made. The following are the general deposit requirements as set forth in the statute:

Unpublished Work: Deposit one complete copy (or phonorecord).

Published Work: Deposit two complete copies (or phonorecords) of the best edition.

Work First Published Outside the United States: Deposit one complete copy (or phonorecord) of the first foreign edition.

Contribution to a Collective Work: Deposit one complete copy (or phonorecord) of the best edition of the collective work.

The Copyright Notice: For published works, the law provides that a copyright notice in a specified form "shall be placed on all publicly distributed copies from which the work can be visually perceived." Use of the copyright notice is the responsibility of the copyright owner and does not require advance permission from the Copyright Office. The required form of the notice for copies generally consists of three elements: (1) the symbol "©", or the word "Copyright," or the abbreviation "Copr."; (2) the year of first publication; and (3) the name of the owner of copyright. For example: "© 1981 Constance Porter." The notice is to be affixed to the copies "in such manner and location as to give reasonable notice of the claim of copyright."

For further information about copyright registration, notice, or special questions relating to copyright problems, write:

Information and Publications Section, LM-455
Copyright Office
Library of Congress
Washington, D.C. 20559

PRIVACY ACT ADVISORY STATEMENT Required by the Privacy Act of 1974 (Public Law 93-579)

AUTHORITY FOR REQUESTING THIS INFORMATION:
• Title 17, U.S.C., Secs. 409 and 410

FURNISHING THE REQUESTED INFORMATION IS:
• Voluntary

BUT IF THE INFORMATION IS NOT FURNISHED:
• It may be necessary to delay or refuse registration
• You may not be entitled to certain relief, remedies, and benefits provided in chapters 4 and 5 of title 17, U.S.C.

PRINCIPAL USES OF REQUESTED INFORMATION:
• Establishment and maintenance of a public record
• Examination of the application for compliance with legal requirements

OTHER ROUTINE USES:
• Public inspection and copying
• Preparation of public indexes
• Preparation of public catalogs of copyright registrations
• Preparation of search reports upon request

NOTE:
• No other advisory statement will be given you in connection with this application
• Please keep this statement and refer to it if we communicate with you regarding this application

LINE-BY-LINE INSTRUCTIONS

1 SPACE 1: Title

Title of This Work: Every work submitted for copyright registration must be given a title to identify that particular work. If the copies or phonorecords of the work bear a title (or an identifying phrase that could serve as a title), transcribe that wording *completely* and *exactly* on the application. Indexing of the registration and future identification of the work will depend on the information you give here.

Previous or Alternative Titles: Complete this space if there are any additional titles for the work under which someone searching for the registration might be likely to look, or under which a document pertaining to the work might be recorded.

Publication as a Contribution: If the work being registered is a contribution to a periodical, serial, or collection, give the title of the contribution in the "Title of this Work" space. Then, in the line headed "Publication as a Contribution," give information about the collective work in which the contribution appeared.

2 SPACE 2: Author(s)

General Instructions: After reading these instructions, decide who are the "authors" of this work for copyright purposes. Then, unless the work is a "collective work," give the requested information about every "author" who contributed any appreciable amount of copyrightable matter to this version of the work. If you need further space, request additional Continuation sheets. In the case of a collective work, such as an anthology, collection of essays, or encyclopedia, give information about the author of the collective work as a whole.

Name of Author: The fullest form of the author's name should be given. Unless the work was "made for hire," the individual who actually created the work is its "author." In the case of a work made for hire, the statute provides that "the employer or other person for whom the work was prepared is considered the author."

What is a "Work Made for Hire"? A "work made for hire" is defined as: (1) "a work prepared by an employee within the scope of his or her employment"; or (2) "a work specially ordered or commissioned for use as a contribution to a collective work, as a part of a motion picture or other audiovisual work, as a translation, as a supplementary work, as a compilation, as an instructional text, as a test, as answer material for a test, or as an atlas, if the parties expressly agree in a written instrument signed by them that the work shall be considered a work made for hire." If you have checked "Yes" to indicate that the work was "made for hire," you must give the full legal name of the employer (or other person for whom the work was prepared). You may also include the name of the employee along with the name of the employer (for example: "Elster Publishing Co., employer for hire of John Ferguson").

"Anonymous" or "Pseudonymous" Work: An author's contribution to a work is "anonymous" if that author is not identified on the copies or phonorecords of the work. An author's contribution to a work is "pseudonymous" if that author is identified on the copies or phonorecords under a fictitious name. If the work is "anonymous" you may: (1) leave the line blank; or (2) state "anonymous" on the line; or (3) reveal the author's identity. If the work is "pseudonymous" you may: (1) leave the line blank; or (2) give the pseudonym and identify it as such (for example: "Huntley Haverstock, pseudonym"); or (3) reveal the author's name, making clear which is the real name and which is the pseudonym (for example: "Judith Barton, whose pseudonym is Madeline Elster"). However, the citizenship or domicile of the author **must** be given in all cases.

Dates of Birth and Death: If the author is dead, the statute requires that the year of death be included in the application unless the work is anonymous or pseudonymous. The author's birth date is optional, but is useful as a form of identification. Leave this space blank if the author's contribution was a "work made for hire."

Author's Nationality or Domicile: Give the country of which the author is a citizen, or the country in which the author is domiciled. Nationality or domicile **must** be given in all cases.

Nature of Authorship: After the words "Nature of Authorship" give a brief general statement of the nature of this particular author's contribution to the work. Examples: "Entire text"; "Coauthor of entire text"; "Chapters 11-14"; "Editorial revisions"; "Compilation and English translation"; "New text."

3 SPACE 3: Creation and Publication

General Instructions: Do not confuse "creation" with "publication." Every application for copyright registration must state "the year in which creation of the work was completed." Give the date and nation of first publication only if the work has been published.

Creation: Under the statute, a work is "created" when it is fixed in a copy or phonorecord for the first time. Where a work has been prepared over a period of time, the part of the work existing in fixed form on a particular date constitutes the created work on that date. The date you give here should be the year in which the author completed the particular version for which registration is now being sought, even if other versions exist or if further changes or additions are planned.

Publication: The statute defines "publication" as "the distribution of copies or phonorecords of a work to the public by sale or other transfer of ownership, or by rental, lease, or lending"; a work is also "published" if there has been an "offering to distribute copies or phonorecords to a group of persons for purposes of further distribution, public performance, or public display." Give the full date (month, day, year) when, and the country where, publication first occurred. If first publication took place simultaneously in the United States and other countries, it is sufficient to state "U.S.A."

4 SPACE 4: Claimant(s)

Name(s) and Address(es) of Copyright Claimant(s): Give the name(s) and address(es) of the copyright claimant(s) in this work even if the claimant is the same as the author. Copyright in a work belongs initially to the author of the work (including, in the case of a work made for hire, the employer or other person for whom the work was prepared). The copyright claimant is either the author of the work or a person or organization to whom the copyright initially belonging to the author has been transferred.

Transfer: The statute provides that, if the copyright claimant is not the author, the application for registration must contain "a brief statement of how the claimant obtained ownership of the copyright." If any copyright claimant named in space 4 is not an author named in space 2, give a brief, general statement summarizing the means by which that claimant obtained ownership of the copyright. Examples: "By written contract"; "Transfer of all rights by author"; "Assignment"; "By will." Do not attach transfer documents or other attachments or riders.

5 SPACE 5: Previous Registration

General Instructions: The questions in space 5 are intended to find out whether an earlier registration has been made for this work and, if so, whether there is any basis for a new registration. As a general rule, only one basic copyright registration can be made for the same version of a particular work.

Same Version: If this version is substantially the same as the work covered by a previous registration, a second registration is not generally possible unless: (1) the work has been registered in unpublished form and a second registration is now being sought to cover this first published edition; or (2) someone other than the author is identified as copyright claimant in the earlier registration, and the author is now seeking registration in his or her own name. If either of these two exceptions apply, check the appropriate box and give the earlier registration number and date. Otherwise, do not submit Form TX; instead, write the Copyright Office for information about supplementary registration or recordation of transfers of copyright ownership.

Changed Version: If the work has been changed, and you are now seeking registration to cover the additions or revisions, check the last box in space 5, give the earlier registration number and date, and complete both parts of space 6 in accordance with the instructions below.

Previous Registration Number and Date: If more than one previous registration has been made for the work, give the number and date of the latest registration.

6 SPACE 6: Derivative Work or Compilation

General Instructions: Complete space 6 if this work is a "changed version," "compilation," or "derivative work," and if it incorporates one or more earlier works that have already been published or registered for copyright, or that have fallen into the public domain. A "compilation" is defined as "a work formed by the collection and assembling of preexisting materials or of data that are selected, coordinated, or arranged in such a way that the resulting work as a whole constitutes an original work of authorship." A "derivative work" is "a work based on one or more preexisting works." Examples of derivative works include translations, fictionalizations, abridgments, condensations, or "any other form in which a work may be recast, transformed, or adapted." Derivative works also include works "consisting of editorial revisions, annotations, or other modifications" if these changes, as a whole, represent an original work of authorship.

Preexisting Material (space 6a): For derivative works, complete this space and space 6b. In space 6a identify the preexisting work that has been recast, transformed, or adapted. An example of preexisting material might be: "Russian version of Goncharov's 'Oblomov'." Do not complete space 6a for compilations.

Material Added to This Work (space 6b): Give a brief, general statement of the new material covered by the copyright claim for which registration is sought. **Derivative work** examples include: "Foreword, editing, critical annotations"; "Translation"; "Chapters 11-17." If the work is a **compilation**, describe both the compilation itself and the material that has been compiled. Example: "Compilation of certain 1917 Speeches by Woodrow Wilson." A work may be both a derivative work and compilation, in which case a sample statement might be: "Compilation and additional new material."

7 SPACE 7: Manufacturing Provisions

General Instructions: The copyright statute currently provides, as a general rule, that the copies of a published work "consisting preponderantly of non-dramatic literary material in the English language" be manufactured in the United States or Canada in order to be lawfully imported and publicly distributed in the United States. If the work being registered is unpublished or not in English, leave this space blank. Complete this space if registration is sought for a published work "consisting preponderantly of nondramatic literary material that is in the English language." Identify those who manufactured the copies and where those manufacturing processes were performed. As an exception to the manufacturing provisions, the statute prescribes that, where manufacture has taken place outside the United States or Canada, a maximum of 2000 copies of the foreign edition may be imported into the United States without affecting the copyright owners' rights. For this purpose, the Copyright Office will issue an Import Statement upon request and payment of a fee of $3 at the time of registration or at any later time. For further information about import statements, write for Form IS.

8 SPACE 8: Reproduction for Use of Blind or Physically Handicapped Individuals

General Instructions: One of the major programs of the Library of Congress is to provide Braille editions and special recordings of works for the exclusive use of the blind and physically handicapped. In an effort to simplify and speed up the copyright licensing procedures that are a necessary part of this program, section 710 of the copyright statute provides for the establishment of a voluntary licensing system to be tied in with copyright registration. Copyright Office regulations provide that you may grant a license for such reproduction and distribution solely for the use of persons who are certified by competent authority as unable to read normal printed material as a result of physical limitations. The license is entirely voluntary, nonexclusive, and may be terminated upon 90 days notice.

How to Grant the License: If you wish to grant it, check one of the three boxes in space 8. Your check in one of these boxes, together with your signature in space 10, will mean that the Library of Congress can proceed to reproduce and distribute under the license without further paperwork. For further information, write for Circular R63.

9,10,11 SPACE 9, 10, 11: Fee, Correspondence, Certification, Return Address

Deposit Account: If you maintain a Deposit Account in the Copyright Office, identify it in space 9. Otherwise leave the space blank and send the fee of $10 with your application and deposit.

Correspondence (space 9): This space should contain the name, address, area code, and telephone number of the person to be consulted if correspondence about this application becomes necessary.

Certification (space 10): The application can not be accepted unless it bears the date and the **handwritten signature** of the author or other copyright claimant, or of the owner of exclusive right(s), or of the duly authorized agent of author, claimant, or owner of exclusive right(s).

Address for Return of Certificate (space 11): The address box must be completed legibly since the certificate will be returned in a window envelope.

FORM TX
UNITED STATES COPYRIGHT OFFICE

REGISTRATION NUMBER

_____

| TX | TXU |

EFFECTIVE DATE OF REGISTRATION

_____

Month   Day   Year

DO NOT WRITE ABOVE THIS LINE. IF YOU NEED MORE SPACE, USE A SEPARATE CONTINUATION SHEET.

1

TITLE OF THIS WORK ▼

PREVIOUS OR ALTERNATIVE TITLES ▼

PUBLICATION AS A CONTRIBUTION If this work was published as a contribution to a periodical, serial, or collection, give information about the collective work in which the contribution appeared. **Title of Collective Work ▼**

If published in a periodical or serial give: **Volume ▼**   **Number ▼**   **Issue Date ▼**   **On Pages ▼**

2

a

NAME OF AUTHOR ▼

DATES OF BIRTH AND DEATH
Year Born ▼   Year Died ▼

Was this contribution to the work a "work made for hire"?
☐ Yes
☐ No

AUTHOR'S NATIONALITY OR DOMICILE
Name of Country
OR { Citizen of ▶ _____
Domiciled in ▶ _____

WAS THIS AUTHOR'S CONTRIBUTION TO THE WORK
Anonymous? ☐ Yes ☐ No
Pseudonymous? ☐ Yes ☐ No
If the answer to either of these questions is "Yes," see detailed instructions.

NATURE OF AUTHORSHIP Briefly describe nature of the material created by this author in which copyright is claimed. ▼

NOTE

Under the law, the "author" of a "work made for hire" is generally the employer, not the employee (see instructions). For any part of this work that was "made for hire" check "Yes" in the space provided, give the employer (or other person for whom the work was prepared) as "Author" of that part, and leave the space for dates of birth and death blank.

b

NAME OF AUTHOR ▼

DATES OF BIRTH AND DEATH
Year Born ▼   Year Died ▼

Was this contribution to the work a "work made for hire"?
☐ Yes
☐ No

AUTHOR'S NATIONALITY OR DOMICILE
Name of country
OR { Citizen of ▶ _____
Domiciled in ▶ _____

WAS THIS AUTHOR'S CONTRIBUTION TO THE WORK
Anonymous? ☐ Yes ☐ No
Pseudonymous? ☐ Yes ☐ No
If the answer to either of these questions is "Yes," see detailed instructions.

NATURE OF AUTHORSHIP Briefly describe nature of the material created by this author in which copyright is claimed. ▼

c

NAME OF AUTHOR ▼

DATES OF BIRTH AND DEATH
Year Born ▼   Year Died ▼

Was this contribution to the work a "work made for hire"?
☐ Yes
☐ No

AUTHOR'S NATIONALITY OR DOMICILE
Name of Country
OR { Citizen of ▶ _____
Domiciled in ▶ _____

WAS THIS AUTHOR'S CONTRIBUTION TO THE WORK
Anonymous? ☐ Yes ☐ No
Pseudonymous? ☐ Yes ☐ No
If the answer to either of these questions is "Yes," see detailed instructions.

NATURE OF AUTHORSHIP Briefly describe nature of the material created by this author in which copyright is claimed. ▼

3

YEAR IN WHICH CREATION OF THIS WORK WAS COMPLETED This information must be given in all cases. ◀ Year

DATE AND NATION OF FIRST PUBLICATION OF THIS PARTICULAR WORK
Complete this information ONLY if this work has been published.
Month ▶ _____ Day ▶ _____ Year ▶ _____ ◀ Nation

4

See instructions before completing this space.

COPYRIGHT CLAIMANT(S) Name and address must be given even if the claimant is the same as the author given in space 2.▼

TRANSFER If the claimant(s) named here in space 4 are different from the author(s) named in space 2, give a brief statement of how the claimant(s) obtained ownership of the copyright.▼

DO NOT WRITE HERE OFFICE USE ONLY

APPLICATION RECEIVED

ONE DEPOSIT RECEIVED

TWO DEPOSITS RECEIVED

REMITTANCE NUMBER AND DATE

MORE ON BACK ▶
- Complete all applicable spaces (numbers 5-11) on the reverse side of this page.
- See detailed instructions.
- Sign the form at line 10.

DO NOT WRITE HERE

Page 1 of _____ pages

EXAMINED BY _____

CHECKED BY _____

☐ CORRESPONDENCE
  Yes

☐ DEPOSIT ACCOUNT
  FUNDS USED

FORM TX

FOR
COPYRIGHT
OFFICE
USE
ONLY

DO NOT WRITE ABOVE THIS LINE. IF YOU NEED MORE SPACE, USE A SEPARATE CONTINUATION SHEET.

PREVIOUS REGISTRATION Has registration for this work, or for an earlier version of this work, already been made in the Copyright Office?

☐ Yes ☐ No If your answer is "Yes," why is another registration being sought? (Check appropriate box) ▼

☐ This is the first published edition of a work previously registered in unpublished form.

☐ This is the first application submitted by this author as copyright claimant.

☐ This is a changed version of the work, as shown by space 6 on this application.

If your answer is "Yes," give: **Previous Registration Number** ▼   **Year of Registration** ▼

5

DERIVATIVE WORK OR COMPILATION Complete both space 6a & 6b for a derivative work; complete only 6b for a compilation.

a. Preexisting Material Identify any preexisting work or works that this work is based on or incorporates. ▼

b. Material Added to This Work Give a brief, general statement of the material that has been added to this work and in which copyright is claimed. ▼

6

See instructions
before completing
this space.

MANUFACTURERS AND LOCATIONS If this is a published work consisting preponderantly of nondramatic literary material in English, the law may require that the copies be manufactured in the United States or Canada for full protection. If so, the names of the manufacturers who performed certain processes, and the places where these processes were performed **must** be given. See instructions for details.

Names of Manufacturers ▼   **Places of Manufacture** ▼

7

REPRODUCTION FOR USE OF BLIND OR PHYSICALLY HANDICAPPED INDIVIDUALS A signature on this form at space 10, and a check in one of the boxes here in space 8, constitutes a non-exclusive grant of permission to the Library of Congress to reproduce and distribute solely for the blind and physically handicapped and under the conditions and limitations prescribed by the regulations of the Copyright Office: (1) copies of the work identified in space 1 of this application in Braille (or similar tactile symbols); or (2) phonorecords embodying a fixation of a reading of that work; or (3) both.

    a ☐ Copies and Phonorecords   **b** ☐ Copies Only   **c** ☐ Phonorecords Only

8

See instructions.

DEPOSIT ACCOUNT If the registration fee is to be charged to a Deposit Account established in the Copyright Office, give name and number of Account.

Name ▼   **Account Number** ▼

9

CORRESPONDENCE Give name and address to which correspondence about this application should be sent. Name/Address/Apt/City/State/Zip ▼

             Area Code & Telephone Number ▶

Be sure to
give your
daytime phone
◀ number.

CERTIFICATION* I, the undersigned, hereby certify that I am the

        Check one ▶

☐ author
☐ other copyright claimant
☐ owner of exclusive right(s)
☐ authorized agent of _____

of the work identified in this application and that the statements made by me in this application are correct to the best of my knowledge.

    Name of author or other copyright claimant, or owner of exclusive right(s) ▲

10

Typed or printed name and date ▼ If this is a published work, this date must be the same as or later than the date of publication given in space 3.

_____ date ▶ _____

Handwritten signature (X) ▼

MAIL CERTIFICATE TO

Certificate will be mailed in window envelope

Name ▼

Number/Street/Apartment Number ▼

City/State/ZIP ▼

Have you:
• Completed all necessary spaces?
• Signed your application in space 10?
• Enclosed check or money order for $10 payable to *Register of Copyrights*?
• Enclosed your deposit material with the application and fee?

MAIL TO: Register of Copyrights, Library of Congress, Washington, D.C. 20559.

11

* 17 U.S.C. § 506(e): Any person who knowingly makes a false representation of a material fact in the application for copyright registration provided for by section 409, or in any written statement filed in connection with the application, shall be fined not more than $2,500.

☆U.S. GOVERNMENT PRINTING OFFICE: 1985: 491-560/20,011   December 1985—200,000

Filling Out Application Form PA

Detach and read these instructions before completing this form. Make sure all applicable spaces have been filled in before you return this form.

BASIC INFORMATION

When to Use This Form: Use Form PA for registration of published or unpublished works of the performing arts. This class includes works prepared for the purpose of being "performed" directly before an audience or indirectly "by means of any device or process." Works of the performing arts include: (1) musical works, including any accompanying words; (2) dramatic works, including any accompanying music; (3) pantomimes and choreographic works; and (4) motion pictures and other audiovisual works.

Deposit to Accompany Application: An application for copyright registration must be accompanied by a deposit consisting of copies or phonorecords representing the entire work for which registration is to be made. The following are the general deposit requirements as set forth in the statute:

Unpublished Work: Deposit one complete copy (or phonorecord).

Published Work: Deposit two complete copies (or phonorecords) of the best edition.

Work First Published Outside the United States: Deposit one complete copy (or phonorecord) of the first foreign edition.

Contribution to a Collective Work: Deposit one complete copy (or phonorecord) of the best edition of the collective work.

Motion Pictures: Deposit *both* of the following: (1) a separate written description of the contents of the motion picture; and (2) for a published work, one complete copy of the best edition of the motion picture; or, for an unpublished work, one complete copy of the motion picture or identifying material. Identifying material may be either an audiorecording of the entire soundtrack or one frame enlargement or similar visual print from each 10-minute segment.

The Copyright Notice: For published works, the law provides that a copyright notice in a specified form "shall be placed on all publicly distributed copies from which the work can be visually perceived." Use of the copyright notice is the responsibility of the copyright owner and does not require advance permission from the Copyright Office. The required form of the notice for copies generally consists of three elements: (1) the symbol "©", or the word "Copyright," or the abbreviation "Copr."; (2) the year of first publication; and (3) the name of the owner of copyright. For example: "© 1981 Constance Porter." The notice is to be affixed to the copies "in such manner and location as to give reasonable notice of the claim of copyright."

For further information about copyright registration, notice, or special questions relating to copyright problems, write:

Information and Publications Section, LM-455
Copyright Office
Library of Congress
Washington, D.C. 20559

PRIVACY ACT ADVISORY STATEMENT Required by the Privacy Act of 1974 (P.L. 93-579)
The authority for requesting this information is title 17, U.S.C., secs. 409 and 410. Furnishing the requested information is voluntary. But if the information is not furnished, it may be necessary to delay or refuse registration and you may not be entitled to certain relief, remedies, and benefits provided in chapters 4 and 5 of title 17, U.S.C.
The principal uses of the requested information are the establishment and maintenance of a public record and the examination of the application for compliance with legal requirements.
Other routine uses include public inspection and copying, preparation of public indexes, preparation of public catalogs of copyright registrations, and preparation of search reports upon request.
NOTE: No other advisory statement will be given in connection with this application. Please keep this statement and refer to it if we communicate with you regarding this application.

LINE-BY-LINE INSTRUCTIONS

1 SPACE 1: Title

Title of This Work: Every work submitted for copyright registration must be given a title to identify that particular work. If the copies or phonorecords of the work bear a title (or an identifying phrase that could serve as a title), transcribe that wording *completely* and *exactly* on the application. Indexing of the registration and future identification of the work will depend on the information you give here. If the work you are registering is an entire "collective work" (such as a collection of plays or songs), give the overall title of the collection. If you are registering one or more individual contributions to a collective work, give the title of each contribution, followed by the title of the collection. Example: "'A Song for Elinda' in *Old and New Ballads for Old and New People.*"

Previous or Alternative Titles: Complete this space if there are any additional titles for the work under which someone searching for the registration might be likely to look, or under which a document pertaining to the work might be recorded.

Nature of This Work: Briefly describe the general nature or character of the work being registered for copyright. Examples: "Music"; "Song Lyrics"; "Words and Music"; "Drama"; "Musical Play"; "Choreography"; "Pantomime"; "Motion Picture"; "Audiovisual Work."

2 SPACE 2: Author(s)

General Instructions: After reading these instructions, decide who are the "authors" of this work for copyright purposes. Then, unless the work is a "collective work," give the requested information about every "author" who contributed any appreciable amount of copyrightable matter to this version of the work. If you need further space, request additional Continuation Sheets. In the case of a collective work, such as a songbook or a collection of plays, give information about the author of the collective work as a whole.

Name of Author: The fullest form of the author's name should be given. Unless the work was "made for hire," the individual who actually created the work is its "author." In the case of a work made for hire, the statute provides that "the employer or other person for whom the work was prepared is considered the author."

What is a "Work Made for Hire"? A "work made for hire" is defined as: (1) "a work prepared by an employee within the scope of his or her employment"; or (2) "a work specially ordered or commissioned for use as a contribution to a collective work, as a part of a motion picture or other audiovisual work, as a translation, as a supplementary work, as a compilation, as an instructional text, as a test, as answer material for a test, or as an atlas, if the parties expressly agree in a written instrument signed by them that the work shall be considered a work made for hire." If you have checked "Yes" to indicate that the work was "made for hire," you must give the full legal name of the employer (or other person for whom the work was prepared). You may also include the name of the employee along with the name of the employer (for example: "Elster Music Co., employer for hire of John Ferguson").

"Anonymous" or "Pseudonymous" Work: An author's contribution to a work is "anonymous" if that author is not identified on the copies or phonorecords of the work. An author's contribution to a work is "pseudonymous" if that author is identified on the copies or phonorecords under a fictitious name. If the work is "anonymous" you may: (1) leave the line blank; or (2) state "anonymous" on the line; or (3) reveal the author's identity. If the work is "pseudonymous" you may: (1) leave the line blank; or (2) give the pseudonym and identify it as such (for example: "Huntley Haverstock, pseudonym"); or (3) reveal the author's name, making clear which is the real name and which is the pseudonym (for example: "Judith Barton, whose pseudonym is Madeline Elster"). However, the citizenship or domicile of the author **must** be given in all cases.

Dates of Birth and Death: If the author is dead, the statute requires that the year of death be included in the application unless the work is anonymous or pseudonymous. The author's birth date is optional, but is useful as a form of identification. Leave this space blank if the author's contribution was a "work made for hire."

Author's Nationality or Domicile: Give the country of which the author is a citizen, or the country in which the author is domiciled. Nationality or domicile **must** be given in all cases.

Nature of Authorship: Give a brief general statement of the nature of this particular author's contribution to the work. Examples: "Words"; "Co-Author of Music"; "Words and Music"; "Arrangement"; "Co-Author of Book and Lyrics"; "Dramatization"; "Screen Play"; "Compilation and English Translation"; "Editorial Revisions."

3 SPACE 3: Creation and Publication

General Instructions: Do not confuse "creation" with "publication." Every application for copyright registration must state "the year in which creation of the work was completed." Give the date and nation of first publication only if the work has been published.

Creation: Under the statute, a work is "created" when it is fixed in a copy or phonorecord for the first time. Where a work has been prepared over a period of time, the part of the work existing in fixed form on a particular date constitutes the created work on that date. The date you give here should be the year in which the author completed the particular version for which registration is now being sought, even if other versions exist or if further changes or additions are planned.

Publication: The statute defines "publication" as "the distribution of copies or phonorecords of a work to the public by sale or other transfer of ownership, or by rental, lease, or lending"; a work is also "published" if there has been an "offering to distribute copies or phonorecords to a group of persons for purposes of further distribution, public performance, or public display." Give the full date (month, day, year) when, and the country where, publication first occurred. If first publication took place simultaneously in the United States and other countries, it is sufficient to state "U.S.A."

4 SPACE 4: Claimant(s)

Name(s) and Address(es) of Copyright Claimant(s): Give the name(s) and address(es) of the copyright claimant(s) in this work even if the claimant is the same as the author. Copyright in a work belongs initially to the author of the work (including, in the case of a work made for hire, the employer or other person for whom the work was prepared). The copyright claimant is either the author of the work or a person or organization to whom the copyright initially belonging to the author has been transferred.

Transfer: The statute provides that, if the copyright claimant is not the author, the application for registration must contain "a brief statement of how the claimant obtained ownership of the copyright." If any copyright claimant named in space 4 is not an author named in space 2, give a brief, general statement summarizing the means by which that claimant obtained ownership of the copyright. Examples: "By written contract"; "Transfer of all rights by author"; "Assignment"; "By will." Do not attach transfer documents or other attachments or riders.

5 SPACE 5: Previous Registration

General Instructions: The questions in space 5 are intended to find out whether an earlier registration has been made for this work and, if so, whether there is any basis for a new registration. As a general rule, only one basic copyright registration can be made for the same version of a particular work.

Same Version: If this version is substantially the same as the work covered by a previous registration, a second registration is not generally possible unless: (1) the work has been registered in unpublished form and a second registration is now being sought to cover this first published edition; or (2) someone other than the author is identified as copyright claimant in the earlier registration, and the author is now seeking registration in his or her own name. If either of these two exceptions apply, check the appropriate box and give the

earlier registration number and date. Otherwise, do not submit Form PA; instead, write the Copyright Office for information about supplementary registration or recordation of transfers of copyright ownership.

Changed Version: If the work has been changed, and you are now seeking registration to cover the additions or revisions, check the last box in space 5, give the earlier registration number and date, and complete both parts of space 6 in accordance with the instructions below.

Previous Registration Number and Date: If more than one previous registration has been made for the work, give the number and date of the latest registration.

6 SPACE 6: Derivative Work or Compilation

General Instructions: Complete space 6 if this work is a "changed version," "compilation," or "derivative work," and if it incorporates one or more earlier works that have already been published or registered for copyright, or that have fallen into the public domain. A "compilation" is defined as "a work formed by the collection and assembling of preexisting materials or of data that are selected, coordinated, or arranged in such a way that the resulting work as a whole constitutes an original work of authorship." A "derivative work" is "a work based on one or more preexisting works." Examples of derivative works include musical arrangements, dramatizations, translations, abridgments, condensations, motion picture versions, or "any other form in which a work may be recast, transformed, or adapted." Derivative works also include works "consisting of editorial revisions, annotations, or other modifications" if these changes, as a whole, represent an original work of authorship.

Preexisting Material (space 6a): Complete this space **and** space 6b for derivative works. In this space identify the preexisting work that has been recast, transformed, or adapted. For example, the preexisting material might be: "French version of Hugo's 'Le Roi s'amuse'." Do not complete this space for compilations.

Material Added to This Work (space 6b): Give a brief, general statement of the **additional** new material covered by the copyright claim for which registration is sought. In the case of a derivative work, identify this new material. Examples: "Arrangement for piano and orchestra"; "Dramatization for television"; "New film version"; "Revisions throughout; Act III completely new." If the work is a compilation, give a brief, general statement describing both the material that has been compiled **and** the compilation itself. Example: "Compilation of 19th Century Military Songs."

7,8,9 SPACE 7, 8, 9: Fee, Correspondence, Certification, Return Address

Deposit Account: If you maintain a Deposit Account in the Copyright Office, identify it in space 7. Otherwise leave the space blank and send the fee of $10 with your application and deposit.

Correspondence (space 7): This space should contain the name, address, area code, and telephone number of the person to be consulted if correspondence about this application becomes necessary.

Certification (space 8): The application cannot be accepted unless it bears the date and the **handwritten signature** of the author or other copyright claimant, or of the owner of exclusive right(s), or of the duly authorized agent of the author, claimant, or owner of exclusive right(s).

Address for Return of Certificate (space 9): The address box must be completed legibly since the certificate will be returned in a window envelope.

MORE INFORMATION

How To Register a Recorded Work: If the musical or dramatic work that you are registering has been recorded (as a tape, disk, or cassette), you may choose either copyright application Form PA or Form SR, Performing Arts or Sound Recordings, depending on the purpose of the registration.

Form PA should be used to register the underlying musical composition or dramatic work. Form SR has been developed specifically to register a "sound recording" as defined by the Copyright Act—a work resulting from the "fixation of a series of sounds," separate and distinct from the underlying musical or dramatic work. Form SR should be used when the copyright claim is limited to the sound recording itself. (In one instance, Form SR may also be used to file for a copyright registration for both kinds of works—see (4) below.) Therefore:

(1) File Form PA if you are seeking to register the musical or dramatic work, not the "sound recording," even though what you deposit for copyright purposes may be in the form of a phonorecord.

(2) File Form PA if you are seeking to register the audio portion of an audiovisual work, such as a motion picture soundtrack; these are considered integral parts of the audiovisual work.

(3) File Form SR if you are seeking to register the "sound recording" itself, that is, the work that results from the fixation of a series of musical, spoken, or other sounds, but not the underlying musical or dramatic work.

(4) File Form SR if you are the copyright claimant for both the underlying musical or dramatic work and the sound recording, *and* you prefer to register both on the same form.

(5) File both forms PA and SR if the copyright claimant for the underlying work and sound recording differ, or you prefer to have separate registration for them.

"Copies" and "Phonorecords": To register for copyright, you are required to deposit "copies" or "phonorecords." These are defined as follows:

Musical compositions may be embodied (fixed) in "copies," objects from which a work can be read or visually perceived, directly or with the aid of a machine or device, such as manuscripts, books, sheet music, film, and videotape. They may also be fixed in "phonorecords," objects embodying fixations of sounds, such as tapes and phonograph disks, commonly known as phonograph records. For example, a song (the work to be registered) can be reproduced in sheet music ("copies") or phonograph records ("phonorecords"), or both.

FORM PA
UNITED STATES COPYRIGHT OFFICE

REGISTRATION NUMBER

PA	PAU

EFFECTIVE DATE OF REGISTRATION

Month	Day	Year

DO NOT WRITE ABOVE THIS LINE. IF YOU NEED MORE SPACE, USE A SEPARATE CONTINUATION SHEET.

1

TITLE OF THIS WORK ▼

PREVIOUS OR ALTERNATIVE TITLES ▼

NATURE OF THIS WORK ▼ See instructions

2

a

NAME OF AUTHOR ▼

DATES OF BIRTH AND DEATH
Year Born ▼   Year Died ▼

Was this contribution to the work a "work made for hire"?
☐ Yes
☐ No

AUTHOR'S NATIONALITY OR DOMICILE
Name of Country
OR { Citizen of ▶_____
     Domiciled in ▶_____

WAS THIS AUTHOR'S CONTRIBUTION TO THE WORK
Anonymous? ☐ Yes ☐ No
Pseudonymous? ☐ Yes ☐ No
If the answer to either of these questions is "Yes," see detailed instructions.

NATURE OF AUTHORSHIP Briefly describe nature of the material created by this author in which copyright is claimed. ▼

b

NAME OF AUTHOR ▼

DATES OF BIRTH AND DEATH
Year Born ▼   Year Died ▼

Was this contribution to the work a "work made for hire"?
☐ Yes
☐ No

AUTHOR'S NATIONALITY OR DOMICILE
Name of country
OR { Citizen of ▶_____
     Domiciled in ▶_____

WAS THIS AUTHOR'S CONTRIBUTION TO THE WORK
Anonymous? ☐ Yes ☐ No
Pseudonymous? ☐ Yes ☐ No
If the answer to either of these questions is "Yes," see detailed instructions.

NATURE OF AUTHORSHIP Briefly describe nature of the material created by this author in which copyright is claimed. ▼

c

NAME OF AUTHOR ▼

DATES OF BIRTH AND DEATH
Year Born ▼   Year Died ▼

Was this contribution to the work a "work made for hire"?
☐ Yes
☐ No

AUTHOR'S NATIONALITY OR DOMICILE
Name of Country
OR { Citizen of ▶_____
     Domiciled in ▶_____

WAS THIS AUTHOR'S CONTRIBUTION TO THE WORK
Anonymous? ☐ Yes ☐ No
Pseudonymous? ☐ Yes ☐ No
If the answer to either of these questions is "Yes," see detailed instructions.

NATURE OF AUTHORSHIP Briefly describe nature of the material created by this author in which copyright is claimed. ▼

NOTE

Under the law, the "author" of a "work made for hire" is generally the employer, not the employee (see instructions). For any part of this work that was "made for hire" check "Yes" in the space provided, give the employer (or other person for whom the work was prepared) as "Author" of that part, and leave the space for dates of birth and death blank.

3

YEAR IN WHICH CREATION OF THIS WORK WAS COMPLETED This information must be given in all cases.
◀ Year

DATE AND NATION OF FIRST PUBLICATION OF THIS PARTICULAR WORK
Complete this information ONLY if this work has been published.
Month ▶_____ Day ▶_____ Year ▶_____
◀ Nation

4

COPYRIGHT CLAIMANT(S) Name and address must be given even if the claimant is the same as the author given in space 2.▼

See instructions before completing this space.

TRANSFER If the claimant(s) named here in space 4 are different from the author(s) named in space 2, give a brief statement of how the claimant(s) obtained ownership of the copyright.▼

DO NOT WRITE HERE OFFICE USE ONLY

APPLICATION RECEIVED

ONE DEPOSIT RECEIVED

TWO DEPOSITS RECEIVED

REMITTANCE NUMBER AND DATE

MORE ON BACK ▶
• Complete all applicable spaces (numbers 5-9) on the reverse side of this page.
• See detailed instructions.   • Sign the form at line 8.

DO NOT WRITE HERE

Page 1 of_____pages

EXAMINED BY	FORM PA
CHECKED BY	
☐ CORRESPONDENCE Yes	FOR COPYRIGHT OFFICE USE ONLY
☐ DEPOSIT ACCOUNT FUNDS USED	

DO NOT WRITE ABOVE THIS LINE. IF YOU NEED MORE SPACE, USE A SEPARATE CONTINUATION SHEET.

PREVIOUS REGISTRATION   Has registration for this work, or for an earlier version of this work, already been made in the Copyright Office?

☐ Yes   ☐ No   If your answer is "Yes," why is another registration being sought? (Check appropriate box) ▼

☐ This is the first published edition of a work previously registered in unpublished form.

☐ This is the first application submitted by this author as copyright claimant.

☐ This is a changed version of the work, as shown by space 6 on this application.

If your answer is "Yes," give: **Previous Registration Number** ▼   **Year of Registration** ▼

5

DERIVATIVE WORK OR COMPILATION   Complete both space 6a & 6b for a derivative work; complete only 6b for a compilation.

a. **Preexisting Material**   Identify any preexisting work or works that this work is based on or incorporates. ▼

b. **Material Added to This Work**   Give a brief, general statement of the material that has been added to this work and in which copyright is claimed. ▼

6

See instructions before completing this space.

DEPOSIT ACCOUNT   If the registration fee is to be charged to a Deposit Account established in the Copyright Office, give name and number of Account.
Name ▼   **Account Number** ▼

7

CORRESPONDENCE   Give name and address to which correspondence about this application should be sent.   Name/Address/Apt/City/State/Zip ▼

Area Code & Telephone Number ▶

Be sure to give your daytime phone ◀ number.

CERTIFICATION*   I, the undersigned, hereby certify that I am the

Check only one ▼

☐ author

☐ other copyright claimant

☐ owner of exclusive right(s)

☐ authorized agent of_____
   Name of author or other copyright claimant, or owner of exclusive right(s) ▲

of the work identified in this application and that the statements made
by me in this application are correct to the best of my knowledge.

Typed or printed name and date ▼ If this is a published work, this date must be the same as or later than the date of publication given in space 3.

date ▶ _____

☞   Handwritten signature (X) ▼

8

MAIL CERTIFI-CATE TO

Name ▼

Number/Street/Apartment Number ▼

City/State/ZIP ▼

Certificate will be mailed in window envelope

Have you:
• Completed all necessary spaces?
• Signed your application in space 8?
• Enclosed check or money order for $10 payable to *Register of Copyrights*?
• Enclosed your deposit material with the application and fee?

MAIL TO: Register of Copyrights, Library of Congress, Washington, D.C. 20559.

9

* 17 U.S.C. § 506(e): Any person who knowingly makes a false representation of a material fact in the application for copyright registration provided for by section 409, or in any written statement filed in connection with the application, shall be fined not more than $2,500.

☆U.S. GOVERNMENT PRINTING OFFICE: 1986:181-531/40,014

November 1986—75,000

Filling Out Application Form VA

Detach and read these instructions before completing this form. Make sure all applicable spaces have been filled in before you return this form.

BASIC INFORMATION

When to Use This Form: Use Form VA for copyright registration of published or unpublished works of the visual arts. This category consists of "pictorial, graphic, or sculptural works," including two-dimensional and three-dimensional works of fine, graphic, and applied art, photographs, prints and art reproductions, maps, globes, charts, technical drawings, diagrams, and models.

What Does Copyright Protect? Copyright in a work of the visual arts protects those pictorial, graphic, or sculptural elements that, either alone or in combination, represent an "original work of authorship." The statute declares: "In no case does copyright protection for an original work of authorship extend to any idea, procedure, process, system, method of operation, concept, principle, or discovery, regardless of the form in which it is described, explained, illustrated, or embodied in such work."

Works of Artistic Craftsmanship and Designs: "Works of artistic craftsmanship" are registrable on Form VA, but the statute makes clear that protection extends to "their form" and not to "their mechanical or utilitarian aspects." The "design of a useful article" is considered copyrightable "only if, and only to the extent that, such design incorporates pictorial, graphic, or sculptural features that can be identified separately from, and are capable of existing independently of, the utilitarian aspects of the article."

Labels and Advertisements: Works prepared for use in connection with the sale or advertisement of goods and services are registrable if they contain "original work of authorship." Use Form VA if the copyrightable material in the work you are registering is mainly pictorial or graphic; use Form TX if it consists mainly of text. **NOTE:** Words and short phrases such as names, titles, and slogans cannot be protected by copyright, and the same is true of standard symbols, emblems, and other commonly used graphic designs that are in the public domain. When used commercially, material of that sort can sometimes be protected under state laws of unfair competition or under the Federal trademark laws. For information about trademark registration, write to the Commissioner of Patents and Trademarks, Washington, D.C. 20231.

Deposit to Accompany Application: An application for copyright registration must be accompanied by a deposit consisting of copies representing the entire work for which registration is to be made.

Unpublished Work: Deposit one complete copy.

Published Work: Deposit two complete copies of the best edition.

Work First Published Outside the United States: Deposit one complete copy of the first foreign edition.

Contribution to a Collective Work: Deposit one complete copy of the best edition of the collective work.

The Copyright Notice: For published works, the law provides that a copyright notice in a specified form "shall be placed on all publicly distributed copies from which the work can be visually perceived." Use of the copyright notice is the responsibility of the copyright owner and does not require advance permission from the Copyright Office. The required form of the notice for copies generally consists of three elements: (1) the symbol "©", or the word "Copyright," or the abbreviation "Copr."; (2) the year of first publication; and (3) the name of the owner of copyright. For example: "© 1981 Constance Porter." The notice is to be affixed to the copies "in such manner and location as to give reasonable notice of the claim of copyright."

For further information about copyright registration, notice, or special questions relating to copyright problems, write:
Information and Publications Section, LM-455
Copyright Office, Library of Congress, Washington, D.C. 20559

PRIVACY ACT ADVISORY STATEMENT Required by the Privacy Act of 1974 (P.L. 93-579)
The authority for requesting this information is title 17, U.S.C., secs. 409 and 410. Furnishing the requested information is voluntary. But if the information is not furnished, it may be necessary to delay or refuse registration and you may not be entitled to certain relief, remedies, and benefits provided in chapters 4 and 5 of title 17, U.S.C.
The principal uses of the requested information are the establishment and maintenance of a public record and the examination of the application for compliance with legal requirements.
Other routine uses include public inspection and copying, preparation of public indexes, preparation of public catalogs of copyright registrations, and preparation of search reports upon request.
NOTE: No other advisory statement will be given in connection with this application. Please keep this statement and refer to it if we communicate with you regarding this application.

LINE-BY-LINE INSTRUCTIONS

1 SPACE 1: Title

Title of This Work: Every work submitted for copyright registration must be given a title to identify that particular work. If the copies of the work bear a title (or an identifying phrase that could serve as a title), transcribe that wording *completely* and *exactly* on the application. Indexing of the registration and future identification of the work will depend on the information you give here.

Previous or Alternative Titles: Complete this space if there are any additional titles for the work under which someone searching for the registration might be likely to look, or under which a document pertaining to the work might be recorded.

Publication as a Contribution: If the work being registered is a contribution to a perodical, serial, or collection, give the title of the contribution in the "Title of This Work" space. Then, in the line headed "Publication as a Contribution," give information about the collective work in which the contribution appeared.

Nature of This Work: Briefly describe the general nature or character of the pictorial, graphic, or sculptural work being registered for copyright. Examples: "Oil Painting"; "Charcoal Drawing"; "Etching"; "Sculpture"; "Map"; "Photograph"; "Scale Model"; "Lithographic Print"; "Jewelry Design"; "Fabric Design."

2 SPACE 2: Author(s)

General Instructions: After reading these instructions, decide who are the "authors" of this work for copyright purposes. Then, unless the work is a "collective work," give the requested information about every "author" who contributed any appreciable amount of copyrightable matter to this version of the work. If you need further space, request additional Continuation Sheets. In the case of a collective work, such as a catalog of paintings or collection of cartoons by various authors, give information about the author of the collective work as a whole.

Name of Author: The fullest form of the author's name should be given. Unless the work was "made for hire," the individual who actually created the work is its "author." In the case of a work made for hire, the statute provides that "the employer or other person for whom the work was prepared is considered the author."

What is a "Work Made for Hire"? A "work made for hire" is defined as: (1) "a work prepared by an employee within the scope of his or her employment"; or (2) "a work specially ordered or commissioned for use as a contribution to a collective work, as a part of a motion picture or other audiovisual work, as a translation, as a supplementary work, as a compilation, as an instructional text, as a test, as answer material for a test, or as an atlas, if the parties expressly agree in a written instrument signed by them that the work shall be considered a work made for hire." If you have checked "Yes" to indicate that the work was "made for hire," you must give the full legal name of the employer (or other person for whom the work was prepared). You may also include the name of the employee along with the name of the employer (for example: "Elster Publishing Co., employer for hire of John Ferguson").

"Anonymous" or "Pseudonymous" Work: An author's contribution to a work is "anonymous" if that author is not identified on the copies or phonorecords of the work. An author's contribution to a work is "pseudonymous" if that author is identified on the copies or phonorecords under a fictitious name. If the work is "anonymous" you may: (1) leave the line blank; or (2) state "anonymous" on the line; or (3) reveal the author's identity. If the work is "pseudonymous" you may: (1) leave the line blank; or (2) give the pseudonym and identify it as such (for example: "Huntley Haverstock, pseudonym"); or (3) reveal the author's name, making clear which is the real name and which is the pseudonym (for example: "Henry Leek, whose pseudonym is Priam Farrel"). However, the citizenship or domicile of the author **must** be given in all cases.

Dates of Birth and Death: If the author is dead, the statute requires that the year of death be included in the application unless the work is anonymous or pseudonymous. The author's birth date is optional, but is useful as a form of identification. Leave this space blank if the author's contribution was a "work made for hire."

Author's Nationality or Domicile: Give the country of which the author is a citizen, or the country in which the author is domiciled. Nationality or domicile **must** be given in all cases.

Nature of Authorship: Give a brief general statement of the nature of this particular author's contribution to the work. Examples: "Painting"; "Photograph"; "Silk Screen Reproduction"; "Co-author of Cartographic Material"; "Technical Drawing"; "Text and Artwork."

3 SPACE 3: Creation and Publication

General Instructions: Do not confuse "creation" with "publication." Every application for copyright registration must state "the year in which creation of the work was completed." Give the date and nation of first publication only if the work has been published.

Creation: Under the statute, a work is "created" when it is fixed in a copy or phonorecord for the first time. Where a work has been prepared over a period of time, the part of the work existing in fixed form on a particular date constitutes the created work on that date. The date you give here should be the year in which the author completed the particular version for which registration is now being sought, even if other versions exist or if further changes or additions are planned.

Publication: The statute defines "publication" as "the distribution of copies or phonorecords of a work to the public by sale or other transfer of ownership, or by rental, lease, or lending"; a work is also "published" if there has been an "offering to distribute copies or phonorecords to a group of persons for purposes of further distribution, public performance, or public display." Give the full date (month, day, year) when, and the country where, publication first occurred. If first publication took place simultaneously in the United States and other countries, it is sufficient to state "U.S.A."

4 SPACE 4: Claimant(s)

Name(s) and Address(es) of Copyright Claimant(s): Give the name(s) and address(es) of the copyright claimant(s) in this work even if the claimant is the same as the author. Copyright in a work belongs initially to the author of the work (including, in the case of a work made for hire, the employer or other person for whom the work was prepared). The copyright claimant is either the author of the work or a person or organization to whom the copyright initially belonging to the author has been transferred.

Transfer: The statute provides that, if the copyright claimant is not the author, the application for registration must contain "a brief statement of how the claimant obtained ownership of the copyright." If any copyright claimant named in space 4 is not an author named in space 2, give a brief, general statement summarizing the means by which that claimant obtained ownership of the copyright. Examples: "By written contract"; "Transfer of all rights by author"; "Assignment"; "By will." Do not attach transfer documents or other attachments or riders.

5 SPACE 5: Previous Registration

General Instructions: The questions in space 5 are intended to find out whether an earlier registration has been made for this work and, if so, whether there is any basis for a new registration. As a rule, only one basic copyright registration can be made for the same version of a particular work.

Same Version: If this version is substantially the same as the work covered by a previous registration, a second registration is not generally possible unless: (1) the work has been registered in unpublished form and a second registration is now being sought to cover this first published edition; or (2) some-

one other than the author is identified as copyright claimant in the earlier registration, and the author is now seeking registration in his or her own name. If either of these two exceptions apply, check the appropriate box and give the earlier registration number and date. Otherwise, do not submit Form VA; instead, write the Copyright Office for information about supplementary registration or recordation of transfers of copyright ownership.

Changed Version: If the work has been changed, and you are now seeking registration to cover the additions or revisions, check the last box in space 5, give the earlier registration number and date, and complete both parts of space 6 in accordance with the instructions below.

Previous Registration Number and Date: If more than one previous registration has been made for the work, give the number and date of the latest registration.

6 SPACE 6: Derivative Work or Compilation

General Instructions: Complete space 6 if this work is a "changed version," "compilation," or "derivative work," and if it incorporates one or more earlier works that have already been published or registered for copyright, or that have fallen into the public domain. A "compilation" is defined as "a work formed by the collection and assembling of preexisting materials or of data that are selected, coordinated, or arranged in such a way that the resulting work as a whole constitutes an original work of authorship." A "derivative work" is "a work based on one or more preexisting works." Examples of derivative works include reproductions of works of art, sculptures based on drawings, lithographs based on paintings, maps based on previously published sources, or "any other form in which a work may be recast, transformed, or adapted." Derivative works also include works "consisting of editorial revisions, annotations, or other modifications" if these changes, as a whole, represent an original work of authorship.

Preexisting Material (space 6a): Complete this space **and** space 6b for derivative works. In this space identify the preexisting work that has been recast, transformed, or adapted. Examples of preexisting material might be "Grunewald Altarpiece"; or "19th century quilt design." Do not complete this space for compilations.

Material Added to This Work (space 6b): Give a brief, general statement of the **additional** new material covered by the copyright claim for which registration is sought. In the case of a derivative work, identify this new material. Examples: "Adaptation of design and additional artistic work"; "Reproduction of painting by photolithography"; "Additional cartographic material"; "Compilation of photographs." If the work is a compilation, give a brief, general statement describing both the material that has been compiled **and** the compilation itself. Example: "Compilation of 19th Century Political Cartoons."

7,8,9 SPACE 7, 8, 9: Fee, Correspondence, Certification, Return Address

Deposit Account: If you maintain a Deposit Account in the Copyright Office, identify it in space 7. Otherwise leave the space blank and send the fee of $10 with your application and deposit.

Correspondence (space 7): This space should contain the name, address, area code, and telephone number of the person to be consulted if correspondence about this application becomes necessary.

Certification (space 8): The application cannot be accepted unless it bears the date and the **handwritten signature** of the author or other copyright claimant, or of the owner of exclusive right(s), or of the duly authorized agent of the author, claimant, or owner of exclusive right(s).

Address for Return of Certificate (space 9): The address box must be completed legibly since the certificate will be returned in a window envelope.

MORE INFORMATION

Form of Deposit for Works of the Visual Arts

Exceptions to General Deposit Requirements: As explained on the reverse side of this page, the statutory deposit requirements (generally one copy for unpublished works and two copies for published works) will vary for particular kinds of works of the visual arts. The copyright law authorizes the Register of Copyrights to issue regulations specifying "the administrative classes into which works are to be placed for purposes of deposit and registration, and the nature of the copies or phonorecords to be deposited in the various classes specified." For particular classes, the regulations may require or permit "the deposit of identifying material instead of copies or phonorecords," or "the deposit of only one copy or phonorecord where two would normally be required."

What Should You Deposit? The detailed requirements with respect to the kind of deposit to accompany an application on Form VA are contained in the Copyright

Office Regulations. The following does not cover all of the deposit requirements, but is intended to give you some general guidance.

For an Unpublished Work, the material deposited should represent the entire copyrightable content of the work for which registration is being sought.

For a Published Work, the material deposited should generally consist of two complete copies of the best edition. Exceptions: (1) For certain types of works, one complete copy may be deposited instead of two. These include greeting cards, postcards, stationery, labels, advertisements, scientific drawings, and globes; (2) For most three-dimensional sculptural works, and for certain two-dimensional works, the Copyright Office Regulations require deposit of identifying material (photographs or drawings in a specified form) rather than copies; and (3) Under certain circumstances, for works published in five copies or less or in limited, numbered editions, the deposit may consist of one copy or of identifying reproductions.

FORM VA
UNITED STATES COPYRIGHT OFFICE

REGISTRATION NUMBER

VA   VAU

EFFECTIVE DATE OF REGISTRATION

Month   Day   Year

DO NOT WRITE ABOVE THIS LINE. IF YOU NEED MORE SPACE, USE A SEPARATE CONTINUATION SHEET.

1

TITLE OF THIS WORK ▼

NATURE OF THIS WORK ▼ See instructions

PREVIOUS OR ALTERNATIVE TITLES ▼

PUBLICATION AS A CONTRIBUTION If this work was published as a contribution to a periodical, serial, or collection, give information about the collective work in which the contribution appeared. **Title of Collective Work ▼**

If published in a periodical or serial give: **Volume ▼**   **Number ▼**   **Issue Date ▼**   **On Pages ▼**

2

a

NAME OF AUTHOR ▼

DATES OF BIRTH AND DEATH
Year Born ▼   Year Died ▼

Was this contribution to the work a "work made for hire"?
☐ Yes
☐ No

AUTHOR'S NATIONALITY OR DOMICILE
Name of Country
OR { Citizen of ▶
{ Domiciled in ▶

WAS THIS AUTHOR'S CONTRIBUTION TO THE WORK
Anonymous? ☐ Yes ☐ No
Pseudonymous? ☐ Yes ☐ No
If the answer to either of these questions is "Yes," see detailed instructions.

NATURE OF AUTHORSHIP Briefly describe nature of the material created by this author in which copyright is claimed. ▼

NOTE

Under the law, the "author" of a work made for hire" is generally the employer, not the employee (see instructions). For any part of this work that was "made for hire" check "Yes" in the space provided, give the employer (or other person for whom the work was prepared) as "Author" of that part, and leave the space for dates of birth and death blank.

b

NAME OF AUTHOR ▼

DATES OF BIRTH AND DEATH
Year Born ▼   Year Died ▼

Was this contribution to the work a "work made for hire"?
☐ Yes
☐ No

AUTHOR'S NATIONALITY OR DOMICILE
Name of country
OR { Citizen of ▶
{ Domiciled in ▶

WAS THIS AUTHOR'S CONTRIBUTION TO THE WORK
Anonymous? ☐ Yes ☐ No
Pseudonymous? ☐ Yes ☐ No
If the answer to either of these questions is "Yes," see detailed instructions.

NATURE OF AUTHORSHIP Briefly describe nature of the material created by this author in which copyright is claimed. ▼

c

NAME OF AUTHOR ▼

DATES OF BIRTH AND DEATH
Year Born ▼   Year Died ▼

Was this contribution to the work a "work made for hire"?
☐ Yes
☐ No

AUTHOR'S NATIONALITY OR DOMICILE
Name of Country
OR { Citizen of ▶
{ Domiciled in ▶

WAS THIS AUTHOR'S CONTRIBUTION TO THE WORK
Anonymous? ☐ Yes ☐ No
Pseudonymous? ☐ Yes ☐ No
If the answer to either of these questions is "Yes," see detailed instructions.

NATURE OF AUTHORSHIP Briefly describe nature of the material created by this author in which copyright is claimed. ▼

3

YEAR IN WHICH CREATION OF THIS WORK WAS COMPLETED This information must be given in all cases. ◀ Year

DATE AND NATION OF FIRST PUBLICATION OF THIS PARTICULAR WORK
Complete this information ONLY if this work has been published. Month ▶ _____ Day ▶ _____ Year ▶ _____ ◀ Nation

4

See instructions before completing this space.

COPYRIGHT CLAIMANT(S) Name and address must be given even if the claimant is the same as the author given in space 2.▼

TRANSFER If the claimant(s) named here in space 4 are different from the author(s) named in space 2, give a brief statement of how the claimant(s) obtained ownership of the copyright.▼

DO NOT WRITE HERE OFFICE USE ONLY

APPLICATION RECEIVED

ONE DEPOSIT RECEIVED

TWO DEPOSITS RECEIVED

REMITTANCE NUMBER AND DATE

MORE ON BACK ▶
• Complete all applicable spaces (numbers 5-9) on the reverse side of this page.
• See detailed instructions.
• Sign the form at line 8.

DO NOT WRITE HERE

Page 1 of _____ pages

☐ CORRESPONDENCE
    Yes

☐ DEPOSIT ACCOUNT
    FUNDS USED

FOR
COPYRIGHT
OFFICE
USE
ONLY

DO NOT WRITE ABOVE THIS LINE. IF YOU NEED MORE SPACE, USE A SEPARATE CONTINUATION SHEET.

PREVIOUS REGISTRATION Has registration for this work, or for an earlier version of this work, already been made in the Copyright Office?

☐ **Yes** ☐ **No** If your answer is "Yes," why is another registration being sought? (Check appropriate box) ▼

☐ This is the first published edition of a work previously registered in unpublished form.

☐ This is the first application submitted by this author as copyright claimant.

☐ This is a changed version of the work, as shown by space 6 on this application.

If your answer is "Yes," give: **Previous Registration Number** ▼   **Year of Registration** ▼

5

DERIVATIVE WORK OR COMPILATION   Complete both space 6a & 6b for a derivative work; complete only 6b for a compilation.

a. Preexisting Material   Identify any preexisting work or works that this work is based on or incorporates. ▼

b. Material Added to This Work   Give a brief, general statement of the material that has been added to this work and in which copyright is claimed.▼

6

See instructions
before completing
this space.

DEPOSIT ACCOUNT   If the registration fee is to be charged to a Deposit Account established in the Copyright Office, give name and number of Account.
Name ▼   **Account Number** ▼

7

CORRESPONDENCE   Give name and address to which correspondence about this application should be sent.   Name/Address/Apt/City/State/Zip ▼

Area Code & Telephone Number ▶

Be sure to
give your
daytime phone
◀ number.

CERTIFICATION*   I, the undersigned, hereby certify that I am the

Check only one ▼

☐ author

☐ other copyright claimant

☐ owner of exclusive right(s)

☐ authorized agent of_____
                       Name of author or other copyright claimant, or owner of exclusive right(s) ▲

of the work identified in this application and that the statements made
by me in this application are correct to the best of my knowledge.

Typed or printed name and date ▼ If this is a published work, this date must be the same as or later than the date of publication given in space 3.

_____ date ▶ _____

☞   Handwritten signature (X) ▼

8

**MAIL
CERTIFI-
CATE TO**

Name ▼

Number/Street/Apartment Number ▼

City/State/ZIP ▼

**Certificate
will be
mailed in
window
envelope**

Have you:
● Completed all necessary
  spaces?
● Signed your application in space
  8?
● Enclosed check or money order
  for $10 payable to *Register of
  Copyrights?*
● Enclosed your deposit material
  with the application and fee?

MAIL TO: Register of Copyrights,
Library of Congress, Washington,
D.C. 20559.

9

* 17 U.S.C. § 506(e): Any person who knowingly makes a false representation of a material fact in the application for copyright registration provided for by section 409, or in any written statement filed in
connection with the application, shall be fined not more than $2,500.

☆ U.S. GOVERNMENT PRINTING OFFICE: 1986—491–560/40,010   August 1986—40,000

Filling Out Application Form SE

Detach and read these instructions before completing this form. Make sure all applicable spaces have been filled in before you return this form.

BASIC INFORMATION

When To Use This Form: Use a separate Form SE for registration of each individual issue of a serial, Class SE. A serial is defined as a work issued or intended to be issued in successive parts bearing numerical or chronological designations and intended to be continued indefinitely. This class includes a variety of works: periodicals; newspapers; annuals; the journals, proceedings, transactions, etc., of societies. Do not use Form SE to register an individual contribution to a serial. Request Form TX for such contributions.

Deposit to Accompany Application: An application for copyright registration must be accompanied by a deposit consisting of copies or phonorecords representing the entire work for which registration is to be made. The following are the general deposit requirements as set forth in the statute:

Unpublished Work: Deposit one complete copy (or phonorecord).

Published Work: Deposit two complete copies (or phonorecords) of the best edition.

Work First Published Outside the United States: Deposit one complete copy (or phonorecord) of the first foreign edition.

Mailing Requirements: It is important that you send the application, the deposit copy or copies, and the $10 fee together in the same envelope or package. The Copyright Office cannot process them unless they are received together. Send to: *Register of Copyrights, Library of Congress, Washington, D.C. 20559.*

The Copyright Notice: For published works, the law provides that a copyright notice in a specified form "shall be placed on all publicly distributed copies from which the work can be visually perceived." Use of the copyright notice is the responsibility of the copyright owner and does not require advance permission from the Copyright Office. The required form of the notice for copies generally consists of three elements: (1) the symbol "©"; or the word "Copyright," or the abbreviation "Copr."; (2) the year of first publication; and (3) the name of the owner of copyright. For example: "© 1981 National News Publishers, Inc." The notice is to be affixed to the copies "in such manner and location as to give reasonable notice of the claim of copyright." For further information about copyright registration, notice, or special questions relating to copyright problems, write:

Information and Publications Section, LM-455
Copyright Office, Library of Congress, Washington, D.C. 20559

> **PRIVACY ACT ADVISORY STATEMENT Required by the Privacy Act of 1974 (P.L. 93-579)**
> The authority for requesting this information is title 17, U.S.C., secs. 409 and 410. Furnishing the requested information is voluntary. But if the information is not furnished, it may be necessary to delay or refuse registration and you may not be entitled to certain relief, remedies, and benefits provided in chapters 4 and 5 of title 17, U.S.C.
> The principal uses of the requested information are the establishment and maintenance of a public record and the examination of the application for compliance with legal requirements.
> Other routine uses include public inspection and copying, preparation of public indexes, preparation of public catalogs of copyright registrations, and preparation of search reports upon request.
> NOTE: No other advisory statement will be given in connection with this application. Please keep this statement and refer to it if we communicate with you regarding this application.

LINE-BY-LINE INSTRUCTIONS

1 SPACE 1: Title

Title of This Serial: Every work submitted for copyright registration must be given a title to identify that particular work. If the copies or phonorecords of the work bear a title (or an identifying phrase that could serve as a title), copy that wording *completely* and *exactly* on the application. Give the volume and number of the periodical issue for which you are seeking registration. The "Date on copies" in space 1 should be the date appearing on the actual copies (for example: "June 1981," "Winter 1981"). Indexing of the registration and future identification of the work will depend on the information you give here.

Previous or Alternative Titles: Complete this space only if there are any additional titles for the serial under which someone searching for the registration might be likely to look, or under which a document pertaining to the work might be recorded.

2 SPACE 2: Author(s)

General Instructions: After reading these instructions, decide who are the "authors" of this work for copyright purposes. In the case of a serial issue, the organization which directs the creation of the serial issue as a whole is generally considered the author of the "collective work" (see "Nature of Authorship") whether it employs a staff or uses the efforts of volunteers. Where, however, an individual is independently responsible for the serial issue, name that person as author of the "collective work."

Name of Author: The fullest form of the author's name should be given. In the case of a "work made for hire," the statute provides that "the employer or other person for whom the work was prepared is considered the author." If this issue is a "work made for hire," the author's name will be the full legal name of the hiring organization, corporation, or individual. The title of the periodical should not ordinarily be listed as "author" because the title itself does not usually correspond to a legal entity capable of authorship. When an individual creates an issue of a serial independently and not as an "employee" of an organization or corporation, that individual should be listed as the "author."

Author's Nationality or Domicile: Give the country of which the author is a citizen, or the country in which the author is domiciled. Nationality or domicile must be given in all cases. The citizenship of an organization formed under United States Federal or state law should be stated as "U.S.A."

What is a "Work Made for Hire"? A "work made for hire" is defined as: (1) "a work prepared by an employee within the scope of his or her employment"; or (2) "a work specially ordered or commissioned for use as a contribution to a collective work, as a part of a motion picture or other audiovisual work, as a translation, as a supplementary work, as a compilation, as an instructional text, as a test, as answer material for a test, or as an atlas, if the parties expressly agree in a written instrument signed by them that the work shall be considered a work made for hire." An organization that uses the efforts of volunteers in the creation of a "collective work" (see "Nature of Authorship") may also be considered the author of a "work made for hire" even though those volunteers were not specifically paid by the organization. In the case of a "work made for hire," give the full legal name of the employer and check "Yes" to indicate that the work was made for hire. You may also include the name of the employee along with the name of the employer (for example: "Elster Publishing Co., employer for hire of John Ferguson").

"Anonymous" or "Pseudonymous" Work: Leave this space blank if the serial is a "work made for hire." An author's contribution to a work is "anonymous" if that author is not identified on the copies or phonorecords of the work. An author's contribution to a work is "pseudonymous" if that author is identified on the copies or phonorecords under a fictitious name. If the work is "anonymous" you may: (1) leave the line blank; or (2) state "anonymous" on the line; or (3) reveal the author's identity. If the work is "pseudonymous" you may: (1) leave the line blank; or (2) give the pseudonym and identify it as such (for example: "Huntley Haverstock, pseudonym"); or (3) reveal the author's name, making clear which is the real name and which is the pseudonym (for example: "Judith Barton, whose pseudonym is Madeline Elster"). However, the citizenship or domicile of the author must be given in all cases.

Dates of Birth and Death: Leave this space blank if the author's contribution was a "work made for hire." If the author is dead, the statute requires that the year of death be included in the application unless the work is anonymous or pseudonymous. The author's birth date is optional, but is useful as a form of identification.

Nature of Authorship: Give a brief statement of the nature of the particular author's contribution to the work. If an organization directed, controlled, and supervised the creation of the serial issue as a whole, check the box "collective work." The term "collective work" means that the author is responsible for compilation and editorial revision, and may also be responsible for certain individual contributions to the serial issue. Further examples of "Authorship" which may apply both to organizational and to individual authors are "Entire text"; "Entire text and/or illustrations"; "Editorial revision, compilation, plus additional new material."

3 SPACE 3: Creation and Publication

General Instructions: Do not confuse "creation" with "publication." Every application for copyright registration must state "the year in which creation of the work was completed." Give the date and nation of first publication only if the work has been published.

Creation: Under the statute, a work is "created" when it is fixed in a copy or phonorecord for the first time. Where a work has been prepared over a period of time, the part of the work existing in fixed form on a particular date constitutes the created work on that date. The date you give here should be the year in which this particular issue was completed.

Publication: The statute defines "publication" as "the distribution of copies or phonorecords of a work to the public by sale or other transfer of ownership, or by rental, lease, or lending"; a work is also "published" if there has been an "offering to distribute copies or phonorecords to a group of persons for purposes of further distribution, public performance, or public display." Give the full date (month, day, year) when, and the country where, publication of this particular issue first occurred. If first publication took place simultaneously in the United States and other countries, it is sufficient to state "U.S.A."

4 SPACE 4: Claimant(s)

Name(s) and Address(es) of Copyright Claimant(s): This space must be completed. Give the name(s) and address(es) of the copyright claimant(s) of this work even if the claimant is the same as the author named in space 2. Copyright in a work belongs initially to the author of the work (including, in the case of a work made for hire, the employer or other person for whom the work was prepared). The copyright claimant is either the author of the work or a person or organization to whom the copyright initially belonging to the author has been transferred.

Transfer: The statute provides that, if the copyright claimant is not the author, the application for registration must contain "a brief statement of how the claimant obtained ownership of the copyright." A transfer of copyright ownership (other than one brought about by operation of law) must be in writing. If any copyright claimant named in space 4 is not an author named in space 2, give a brief, general statement describing the means by which that claimant obtained ownership of the copyright from the original author. Examples: "By written contract"; "Written transfer of all rights by author"; "Assignment"; "Inherited by will." Do not attach the actual document of transfer or other attachments or riders.

5 SPACE 5: Previous Registration

General Instructions: This space applies only rarely to serials. Complete space 5 if this particular issue has been registered earlier or if it contains a substantial amount of material that has been previously registered. Do not complete this space if the previous registrations are simply those made for earlier issues.

Previous Registration:
a. **Check this box** if this issue has been registered in unpublished form and a second registration is now sought to cover the first published edition.

b. **Check this box** if someone other than the author is identified as copyright claimant in the earlier registration and the author is now seeking registration in his or her own name. If the work in question is a contribution to a collective work, as opposed to the issue as a whole, file Form TX, not Form SE.

c. **Check this box** (and complete space 6) if this particular issue, or a substantial portion of the material in it, has been previously registered and you are now seeking registration for the additions and revisions which appear in this issue for the first time.

Previous Registration Number and Date: Complete this line if you checked one of the boxes above. If more than one previous registration has been made for the issue or for material in it, give only the number and year date for the latest registration.

6 SPACE 6: Derivative Work or Compilation

General Instructions: Complete space 6 if this issue is a "changed version," "compilation," or "derivative work," which incorporates one or more earlier works that have already been published or registered for copyright, or that have fallen into the public domain. Do not complete space 6 for an issue consisting of entirely new material appearing for the first time, such as a new issue of a continuing serial. A "compilation" is defined as "a work formed by the collection and assembling of preexisting materials or of data that are selected, coordinated, or arranged in such a way that the resulting work as a whole constitutes an original work of authorship." A "derivative work" is "a work based on one or more preexisting works." Examples of derivative works include translations, fictionalizations, abridgments, condensations, or "any other form in which a work may be recast, transformed, or adapted." Derivative works also include works "consisting of editorial revisions, annotations, or other modifications" if these changes, as a whole, represent an original work of authorship.

Preexisting Material (space 6a): For derivative works, complete this space and space 6b. In space 6a identify the preexisting work that has been recast, transformed, adapted, or updated. Example: "1978 Morgan Co. Sales Catalog." Do not complete space 6a for compilations.

Material Added to This Work (space 6b): Give a brief, general statement of the new material covered by the copyright claim for which registration is sought. **Derivative work** examples include: "Editorial revisions and additions to the Catalog"; "Translation"; "Additional material." If a periodical issue is a **compilation**, describe both the compilation itself and the material that has been compiled. Examples: "Compilation of previously published journal articles"; "Compilation of previously published data." An issue may be both a derivative work and a compilation, in which case a sample statement might be: "Compilation of [describe] and additional new material."

7 SPACE 7: Manufacturing Provisions

General Instructions: The copyright statute currently provides, as a general rule, that the copies of a published work "consisting preponderantly of nondramatic literary material in the English language" be manufactured in the United States or Canada in order to be lawfully imported and publicly distributed in the United States. If the work being registered is unpublished or not in English, leave this space blank. Complete this space if registration is sought for a published work "consisting preponderantly of nondramatic literary material that is in the English language." Identify those who manufactured the copies and where those manufacturing processes were performed. As an exception to the manufacturing provisions, the statute prescribes that, where manufacture has taken place outside the United States or Canada, a maximum of 2000 copies of the foreign edition may be imported into the United States without affecting the copyright owners' rights. For this purpose, the Copyright Office will issue an Import Statement upon request and payment of a fee of $3 at the time of registration or at any later time. For further information about import statements, write for Form IS.

8 SPACE 8: Reproduction for Use of Blind or Physically Handicapped Individuals

General Instructions: One of the major programs of the Library of Congress is to provide Braille editions and special recordings of works for the exclusive use of the blind and physically handicapped. In an effort to simplify and speed up the copyright licensing procedures that are a necessary part of this program, section 710 of the copyright statute provides for the establishment of a voluntary licensing system to be tied in with copyright registration. Copyright Office regulations provide that you may grant a license for such reproduction and distribution solely for the use of persons who are certified by competent authority as unable to read normal printed material as a result of physical limitations. The license is entirely voluntary, nonexclusive, and may be terminated upon 90 days notice.

How to Grant the License: If you wish to grant it, check one of the three boxes in space 8. Your check in one of these boxes, together with your signature in space 10, will mean that the Library of Congress can proceed to reproduce and distribute under the license without further paperwork. For further information, write for Circular R63.

9,10,11 SPACE 9, 10, 11: Fee, Correspondence, Certification, Return Address

Deposit Account: If you maintain a Deposit Account in the Copyright Office, identify it in space 9. Otherwise leave the space blank and send the fee of $10 with your application and deposit.

Correspondence (space 9): This space should contain the name, address, area code, and telephone number of the person to be consulted if correspondence about this application becomes necessary.

Certification (space 10): The application cannot be accepted unless it bears the date and the **handwritten signature** of the author or other copyright claimant, or of the owner of exclusive right(s), or of the duly authorized agent of the author, claimant, or owner of exclusive right(s).

Address for Return of Certificate (space 11): The address box must be completed legibly since the certificate will be returned in a window envelope.

FORM SE
UNITED STATES COPYRIGHT OFFICE

REGISTRATION NUMBER

U

EFFECTIVE DATE OF REGISTRATION

Month _____ Day _____ Year _____

DO NOT WRITE ABOVE THIS LINE. IF YOU NEED MORE SPACE, USE A SEPARATE CONTINUATION SHEET.

1

TITLE OF THIS SERIAL ▼

Volume ▼   Number ▼   Date on Copies ▼   Frequency of Publication ▼

PREVIOUS OR ALTERNATIVE TITLES ▼

2

a

NAME OF AUTHOR ▼

DATES OF BIRTH AND DEATH
Year Born ▼   Year Died ▼

Was this contribution to the work a "work made for hire"?
☐ Yes
☐ No

AUTHOR'S NATIONALITY OR DOMICILE
Name of Country
OR { Citizen of ▶ _____
Domiciled in ▶ _____

WAS THIS AUTHOR'S CONTRIBUTION TO THE WORK
Anonymous?   ☐ Yes ☑ No
Pseudonymous? ☐ Yes ☐ No

If the answer to either of these questions is "Yes," see detailed instructions.

NATURE OF AUTHORSHIP Briefly describe nature of the material created by this author in which copyright is claimed. ▼
☐ Collective Work   Other:

NOTE

Under the law, the "author" of a "work made for hire" is generally the employer, not the employee (see instructions). For any part of this work that was "made for hire" check "Yes" in the space provided, give the employer (or other person for whom the work was prepared) as "Author" of that part, and leave the space for dates of birth and death blank.

b

NAME OF AUTHOR ▼

DATES OF BIRTH AND DEATH
Year Born ▼   Year Died ▼

Was this contribution to the work a "work made for hire"?
☐ Yes
☐ No

AUTHOR'S NATIONALITY OR DOMICILE
Name of country
OR { Citizen of ▶ _____
Domiciled in ▶ _____

WAS THIS AUTHOR'S CONTRIBUTION TO THE WORK
Anonymous?   ☐ Yes ☐ No
Pseudonymous? ☐ Yes ☐ No

If the answer to either of these questions is "Yes," see detailed instructions.

NATURE OF AUTHORSHIP Briefly describe nature of the material created by this author in which copyright is claimed. ▼
☐ Collective Work   Other:

c

NAME OF AUTHOR ▼

DATES OF BIRTH AND DEATH
Year Born ▼   Year Died ▼

Was this contribution to the work a "work made for hire"?
☐ Yes
☐ No

AUTHOR'S NATIONALITY OR DOMICILE
Name of Country
OR { Citizen of ▶ _____
Domiciled in ▶ _____

WAS THIS AUTHOR'S CONTRIBUTION TO THE WORK
Anonymous?   ☐ Yes ☐ No
Pseudonymous? ☐ Yes ☐ No

If the answer to either of these questions is "Yes," see detailed instructions.

NATURE OF AUTHORSHIP Briefly describe nature of the material created by this author in which copyright is claimed. ▼
☐ Collective Work   Other:

3

YEAR IN WHICH CREATION OF THIS ISSUE WAS COMPLETED This information must be given in all cases.
◀ Year

DATE AND NATION OF FIRST PUBLICATION OF THIS PARTICULAR ISSUE Complete this information ONLY if this work has been published.
Month ▶ _____ Day ▶ _____ Year ▶ _____
◀ Nation

4

COPYRIGHT CLAIMANT(S) Name and address must be given even if the claimant is the same as the author given in space 2.▼

See instructions before completing this space.

TRANSFER If the claimant(s) named here in space 4 are different from the author(s) named in space 2, give a brief statement of how the claimant(s) obtained ownership of the copyright.▼

DO NOT WRITE HERE OFFICE USE ONLY

APPLICATION RECEIVED

ONE DEPOSIT RECEIVED

TWO DEPOSITS RECEIVED

REMITTANCE NUMBER AND DATE

MORE ON BACK ▶
• Complete all applicable spaces (numbers 5-11) on the reverse side of this page.
• See detailed instructions.
• Sign the form at line 10.

DO NOT WRITE HERE

Page 1 of _____ pages

EXAMINED BY

CHECKED BY

☐ CORRESPONDENCE
  Yes

☐ DEPOSIT ACCOUNT
  FUNDS USED

FORM SE

FOR
COPYRIGHT
OFFICE
USE
ONLY

DO NOT WRITE ABOVE THIS LINE. IF YOU NEED MORE SPACE, USE A SEPARATE CONTINUATION SHEET.

PREVIOUS REGISTRATION Has registration for this issue, or for an earlier version of this particular issue, already been made in the Copyright Office?

☐ Yes ☐ No If your answer is "Yes," why is another registration being sought? (Check appropriate box) ▼

a. ☐ This is the first published version of an issue previously registered in unpublished form.

b. ☐ This is the first application submitted by this author as copyright claimant.

c. ☐ This is a changed version of this issue, as shown by space 6 on this application.

If your answer is "Yes," give: **Previous Registration Number** ▼   **Year of Registration** ▼

5

DERIVATIVE WORK OR COMPILATION Complete both space 6a & 6b for a derivative work; complete only 6b for a compilation.

a. **Preexisting Material** Identify any preexisting work or works that this work is based on or incorporates. ▼

b. **Material Added to This Work** Give a brief, general statement of the material that has been added to this work and in which copyright is claimed. ▼

6

See instructions before completing this space.

MANUFACTURERS AND LOCATIONS If this is a published work consisting preponderantly of nondramatic literary material in English, the law may require that the copies be manufactured in the United States or Canada for full protection. If so, the names of the manufacturers who performed certain processes, and the places where these processes were performed **must** be given. See instructions for details.

Names of Manufacturers ▼   **Places of Manufacture** ▼

7

REPRODUCTION FOR USE OF BLIND OR PHYSICALLY HANDICAPPED INDIVIDUALS A signature on this form at space 10, and a check in one of the boxes here in space 8, constitutes a non-exclusive grant of permission to the Library of Congress to reproduce and distribute solely for the blind and physically handicapped and under the conditions and limitations prescribed by the regulations of the Copyright Office: (1) copies of the work identified in space 1 of this application in Braille (or similar tactile symbols); or (2) phonorecords embodying a fixation of a reading of that work; or (3) both.

a ☐ Copies and Phonorecords   b ☐ Copies Only   c ☐ Phonorecords Only

8

See instructions.

DEPOSIT ACCOUNT If the registration fee is to be charged to a Deposit Account established in the Copyright Office, give name and number of Account.

Name ▼   **Account Number** ▼

9

CORRESPONDENCE Give name and address to which correspondence about this application should be sent.   Name/Address/Apt/City/State/Zip ▼

Area Code & Telephone Number ▶

Be sure to give your daytime phone number. ◀

CERTIFICATION* I, the undersigned, hereby certify that I am the

Check one ▶

☐ author
☐ other copyright claimant
☐ owner of exclusive right(s)
☐ authorized agent of _____

of the work identified in this application and that the statements made by me in this application are correct to the best of my knowledge.

Name of author or other copyright claimant, or owner of exclusive right(s) ▲

10

Typed or printed name and date ▼ If this is a published work, this date must be the same as or later than the date of publication given in space 3.

_____ date ▶ _____

Handwritten signature (X) ▼

MAIL CERTIFICATE TO

Certificate will be mailed in window envelope

Name ▼

Number/Street/Apartment Number ▼

City/State/ZIP ▼

Have you:
• Completed all necessary spaces?
• Signed your application in space 10?
• Enclosed check or money order for $10 payable to *Register of Copyrights*?
• Enclosed your deposit material with the application and fee?

MAIL TO: Register of Copyrights, Library of Congress, Washington, D.C. 20559.

11

* 17 U.S.C. § 506(e): Any person who knowingly makes a false representation of a material fact in the application for copyright registration provided for by section 409, or in any written statement filed in connection with the application, shall be fined not more than $2,500.

☆U.S. GOVERNMENT PRINTING OFFICE: 1985—461-584—20,004

July 1985—50,000

Filling Out Application Form SR

Detach and read these instructions before completing this form. Make sure all applicable spaces have been filled in before you return this form.

BASIC INFORMATION

When to Use This Form: Use Form SR for copyright registration of published or unpublished sound recordings. It should be used where the copyright claim is limited to the sound recording itself, and it may also be used where the same copyright claimant is seeking simultaneous registration of the underlying musical, dramatic, or literary work embodied in the phonorecord.

With one exception, "sound recordings" are works that result from the fixation of a series of musical, spoken, or other sounds. The exception is for the audio portions of audiovisual works, such as a motion picture soundtrack or an audio cassette accompanying a filmstrip; these are considered a part of the audiovisual work as a whole.

Deposit to Accompany Application: An application for copyright registration of a sound recording must be accompanied by a deposit consisting of phonorecords representing the entire work for which registration is to be made.

Unpublished Work: Deposit one complete phonorecord.

Published Work: Deposit two complete phonorecords of the best edition, together with "any printed or other visually perceptible material" published with the phonorecords.

Work First Published Outside the United States: Deposit one complete phonorecord of the first foreign edition.

Contribution to a Collective Work: Deposit one complete phonorecord of the best edition of the collective work.

The Copyright Notice: For published sound recordings, the law provides that a copyright notice in a specified form "shall be placed on all publicly distributed phonorecords of the sound recording." Use of the copyright notice is the responsibility of the copyright owner and does not require advance permission from the Copyright Office. The required form of the notice for phonorecords of sound recordings consists of three elements: (1) the symbol "℗" (the letter "P" in a circle); (2) the year of first publication of the sound recording; and (3) the name of the owner of copyright. For example: "℗ 1981 Rittenhouse Record Co." The notice is to be "placed on the surface of the phonorecord, or on the label or container, in such manner and location as to give reasonable notice of the claim of copyright." For further information about copyright, write:
Information and Publications Section, LM-455
Copyright Office, Library of Congress, Washington, D.C. 20559

PRIVACY ACT ADVISORY STATEMENT Required by the Privacy Act of 1974 (P.L. 93-579)
The authority for requesting this information is title 17, U.S.C., secs. 409 and 410. Furnishing the requested information is voluntary. But if the information is not furnished, it may be necessary to delay or refuse registration and you may not be entitled to certain relief, remedies, and benefits provided in chapters 4 and 5 of title 17, U.S.C.
The principal uses of the requested information are the establishment and maintenance of a public record and the examination of the application for compliance with legal requirements.
Other routine uses include public inspection and copying, preparation of public indexes, preparation of public catalogs of copyright registrations, and preparation of search reports upon request.
NOTE: No other advisory statement will be given in connection with this application. Please keep this statement and refer to it if we communicate with you regarding this application.

LINE-BY-LINE INSTRUCTIONS

SPACE 1: Title

Title of This Work: Every work submitted for copyright registration must be given a title to identify that particular work. If the phonorecords or any accompanying printed material bear a title (or an identifying phrase that could serve as a title), transcribe that wording completely and exactly on the application. Indexing of the registration and future identification of the work may depend on the information you give here.

Nature of Material Recorded: Indicate the general type or character of the works or other material embodied in the recording. The box marked "Literary" should be checked for nondramatic spoken material of all sorts, including narration, interviews, panel discussions, and training material. If the material recorded is not musical, dramatic, or literary in nature, check "Other" and briefly describe the type of sounds fixed in the recording. For example: "Sound Effects"; "Bird Calls"; "Crowd Noises."

Previous or Alternative Titles: Complete this space if there are any additional titles for the work under which someone searching for the registration might be likely to look, or under which a document pertaining to the work might be recorded.

SPACE 2: Author(s)

General Instructions: After reading these instructions, decide who are the authors" of this work for copyright purposes. Then, unless the work is a collective work," give the requested information about every "author" who contributed any appreciable amount of copyrightable matter to this version of the work. If you need further space, request additional Continuation Sheets. In the case of a collective work, such as a collection of previously published or registered sound recordings, give information about the author of the collective work as a whole. If you are submitting this Form SR to cover the recorded musical, dramatic, or literary work as well as the sound recording itself, it is important for space 2 to include full information about the various authors of all of the material covered by the copyright claim, making clear the nature of each author's contribution.

Name of Author: The fullest form of the author's name should be given. Unless the work was "made for hire," the individual who actually created the work is its "author." In the case of a work made for hire, the statute provides that "the employer or other person for whom the work was prepared is considered the author."

What is a "Work Made for Hire"? A "work made for hire" is defined as: (1) "a work prepared by an employee within the scope of his or her employment"; or (2) "a work specially ordered or commissioned for use as a contribution to a collective work, as a part of a motion picture or other audiovisual work, as a translation, as a supplementary work, as a compilation, as an instructional text, as a test, as answer material for a test, or as an atlas, if the parties expressly agree in a written instrument signed by them that the work shall be considered a work made for hire." If you have checked "Yes" to indicate that the work was "made for hire," you must give the full legal name of the employer (or other person for whom the work was prepared). You may also include the name of the employee along with the name of the employer (for example: "Elster Record Co., employer for hire of John Ferguson").

"Anonymous" or "Pseudonymous" Work: An author's contribution to a work is "anonymous" if that author is not identified on the copies or phonorecords of the work. An author's contribution to a work is "pseudonymous" if that author is identified on the copies or phonorecords under a fictitious name. If the work is "anonymous" you may: (1) leave the line blank; or (2) state "anonymous" on the line; or (3) reveal the author's identity. If the work is "pseudonymous" you may: (1) leave the line blank; or (2) give the pseudonym and identify it as such (for example: "Huntley Haverstock, pseudonym"); or (3) reveal the author's name, making clear which is the real name and which is the pseudonym (for example: "Judith Barton, whose pseudonym is Madeline Elster"). However, the citizenship or domicile of the author **must** be given in all cases.

Dates of Birth and Death: If the author is dead, the statute requires that the year of death be included in the application unless the work is anonymous or pseudonymous. The author's birth date is optional, but is useful as a form of identification. Leave this space blank if the author's contribution was a "work made for hire."

Author's Nationality or Domicile: Give the country of which the author is a citizen, or the country in which the author is domiciled. Nationality or domicile **must** be given in all cases.

Nature of Authorship: Give a brief general statement of the nature of this particular author's contribution to the work. If you are submitting this Form SR to cover both the sound recording and the underlying musical, dramatic, or literary work, make sure that the precise nature of each author's contribution is reflected here. Examples where the authorship pertains to the recording: "Sound Recording"; "Performance and Recording"; "Compilation and Remixing of Sounds." Examples where the authorship pertains to both the recording and the underlying work: "Words, Music, Performance, Recording"; "Arrangement of Music and Recording"; "Compilation of Poems and Reading."

3 SPACE 3: Creation and Publication

General Instructions: Do not confuse "creation" with "publication." Every application for copyright registration must state "the year in which creation of the work was completed." Give the date and nation of first publication only if the work has been published.

Creation: Under the statute, a work is "created" when it is fixed in a copy or phonorecord for the first time. Where a work has been prepared over a period of time, the part of the work existing in fixed form on a particular date constitutes the created work on that date. The date you give here should be the year in which the author completed the particular version for which registration is now being sought, even if other versions exist or if further changes or additions are planned.

Publication: The statute defines "publication" as "the distribution of copies or phonorecords of a work to the public by sale or other transfer of ownership, or by rental, lease, or lending"; a work is also "published" if there has been an "offering to distribute copies or phonorecords to a group of persons for purposes of further distribution, public performance, or public display." Give the full date (month, day, year) when, and the country where, publication first occurred. If first publication took place simultaneously in the United States and other countries, it is sufficient to state "U.S.A."

4 SPACE 4: Claimant(s)

Name(s) and Address(es) of Copyright Claimant(s): Give the name(s) and address(es) of the copyright claimant(s) in this work even if the claimant is the same as the author. Copyright in a work belongs initially to the author of the work (including, in the case of a work made for hire, the employer or other person for whom the work was prepared). The copyright claimant is either the author of the work or a person or organization to whom the copyright initially belonging to the author has been transferred.

Transfer: The statute provides that, if the copyright claimant is not the author, the application for registration must contain "a brief statement of how the claimant obtained ownership of the copyright." If any copyright claimant named in space 4 is not an author named in space 2, give a brief, general statement summarizing the means by which that claimant obtained ownership of the copyright. Examples: "By written contract"; "Transfer of all rights by author"; "Assignment"; "By will." Do not attach transfer documents or other attachments or riders.

5 SPACE 5: Previous Registration

General Instructions: The questions in space 5 are intended to find out whether an earlier registration has been made for this work and, if so, whether there is any basis for a new registration. As a rule, only one basic copyright registration can be made for the same version of a particular work.

Same Version: If this version is substantially the same as the work covered by a previous registration, a second registration is not generally possible unless: (1) the work has been registered in unpublished form and a second registration is now being sought to cover this first published edition; or (2) someone other than the author is identified as copyright claimant in the earlier registration, and the author is now seeking registration in his or her own name. If either of these two exceptions apply, check the appropriate box and give the earlier registration number and date. Otherwise, do not submit Form SR; instead, write the Copyright Office for information about supplementary registration or recordation of transfers of copyright ownership.

Changed Version: If the work has been changed, and you are now seeking registration to cover the additions or revisions, check the last box in space 5, give the earlier registration number and date, and complete both parts of space 6 in accordance with the instructions below.

Previous Registration Number and Date: If more than one previous registration has been made for the work, give the number and date of the latest registration.

6 SPACE 6: Derivative Work or Compilation

General Instructions: Complete space 6 if this work is a "changed version," "compilation," or "derivative work," and if it incorporates one or more earlier works that have already been published or registered for copyright, or that have fallen into the public domain, or sound recordings that were fixed before February 15, 1972. A "compilation" is defined as "a work formed by the collection and assembling of preexisting materials or of data that are selected, coordinated, or arranged in such a way that the resulting work as a whole constitutes an original work of authorship." A "derivative work" is "a work based on one or more preexisting works." Examples of derivative works include recordings reissued with substantial editorial revisions or abridgments of the recorded sounds, and recordings republished with new recorded material, or "any other form in which a work may be recast, transformed, or adapted." Derivative works also include works "consisting of editorial revisions, annotations, or other modifications" if these changes, as a whole, represent an original work of authorship.

Preexisting Material (space 6a): Complete this space **and** space 6b for derivative works. In this space identify the preexisting work that has been recast, transformed, or adapted. For example, the preexisting material might be: "1970 recording by Sperryville Symphony of Bach Double Concerto." Do not complete this space for compilations.

Material Added to This Work (space 6b): Give a brief, general statement of the **additional** new material covered by the copyright claim for which registration is sought. In the case of a derivative work, identify this new material. Examples: "Recorded performances on bands 1 and 3"; "Remixed sounds from original multitrack sound sources"; "New words, arrangement, and additional sounds." If the work is a compilation, give a brief, general statement describing both the material that has been compiled **and** the compilation itself. Example: "Compilation of 1938 Recordings by various swing bands."

7,8,9 SPACE 7, 8, 9: Fee, Correspondence, Certification, Return Address

Deposit Account: If you maintain a Deposit Account in the Copyright Office, identify it in space 7. Otherwise leave the space blank and send the fee of $10 with your application and deposit.

Correspondence (space 7): This space should contain the name, address, area code, and telephone number of the person to be consulted if correspondence about this application becomes necessary.

Certification (space 8): The application cannot be accepted unless it bears the date and the **handwritten signature** of the author or other copyright claimant, or of the owner of exclusive right(s), or of the duly authorized agent of the author, claimant, or owner of exclusive right(s).

Address for Return of Certificate (space 9): The address box must be completed legibly since the certificate will be returned in a window envelope.

MORE INFORMATION

"Works": "Works" are the basic subject matter of copyright; they are what authors create and copyright protects. The statute draws a sharp distinction between the "work" and "any material object in which the work is embodied."

"Copies" and "Phonorecords": These are the two types of material objects in which "works" are embodied. In general, **copies** are objects from which a work can be read or visually perceived, directly or with the aid of a machine or device, such as manuscripts, books, sheet music, film, and videotape. **Phonorecords** are objects embodying fixations of sounds, such as audio tapes and phonograph disks. For example, a song (the "work") can be reproduced in sheet music ("copies") or phonograph disks ("phonorecords"), or both.

"Sound Recordings": These are "works," not "copies" or "phonorecords." "Sound recordings" are "works that result from the fixation of a series of musical, spoken, or other sounds, but not including the sounds accompanying a motion picture or other audiovisual work." Example: When a record company issues a new release, the release will typically involve two distinct "works": the "musical work" that has been recorded, and the "sound recording" as a separate work in itself. The material objects that the record company sends out are "phonorecords": physical reproductions of both the "musical work" and the "sound recording."

Should You File More Than One Application? If your work consists of a recorded musical, dramatic, or literary work, and both that "work," and the sound recording as a separate "work," are eligible for registration, the application form you should file depends on the following:

File Only Form SR if: The copyright claimant is the same for both the musical, dramatic, or literary work and for the sound recording, and you are seeking a single registration to cover both of these "works."

File Only Form PA (or Form TX) if: You are seeking to register only the musical, dramatic, or literary work, not the sound recording. Form PA is appropriate for works of the performing arts; Form TX is for nondramatic literary works.

Separate Applications Should Be Filed on Form PA (or Form TX) and on Form SR if: (1) The copyright claimant for the musical, dramatic, or literary work is different from the copyright claimant for the sound recording; or (2) You prefer to have separate registrations for the musical, dramatic, or literary work and for the sound recording.

FORM SR

UNITED STATES COPYRIGHT OFFICE

REGISTRATION NUMBER

_____

SR   SRU

EFFECTIVE DATE OF REGISTRATION

_____

Month   Day   Year

DO NOT WRITE ABOVE THIS LINE. IF YOU NEED MORE SPACE, USE A SEPARATE CONTINUATION SHEET.

1

TITLE OF THIS WORK ▼

PREVIOUS OR ALTERNATIVE TITLES ▼

NATURE OF MATERIAL RECORDED ▼ See instructions.

- ☐ Musical   ☐ Musical-Dramatic
- ☐ Dramatic   ☐ Literary
- ☐ Other _____

2

a

NAME OF AUTHOR ▼

DATES OF BIRTH AND DEATH
Year Born ▼   Year Died ▼

Was this contribution to the work a "work made for hire"?
- ☐ Yes
- ☐ No

AUTHOR'S NATIONALITY OR DOMICILE
Name of Country
OR { Citizen of ▶ _____
     Domiciled in ▶ _____

WAS THIS AUTHOR'S CONTRIBUTION TO THE WORK
Anonymous? ☐ Yes ☐ No
Pseudonymous? ☐ Yes ☐ No

If the answer to either of these questions is "Yes," see detailed instructions.

NATURE OF AUTHORSHIP Briefly describe nature of the material created by this author in which copyright is claimed. ▼

b

NAME OF AUTHOR ▼

DATES OF BIRTH AND DEATH
Year Born ▼   Year Died ▼

Was this contribution to the work a "work made for hire"?
- ☐ Yes
- ☐ No

AUTHOR'S NATIONALITY OR DOMICILE
Name of country
OR { Citizen of ▶ _____
     Domiciled in ▶ _____

WAS THIS AUTHOR'S CONTRIBUTION TO THE WORK
Anonymous? ☐ Yes ☐ No
Pseudonymous? ☐ Yes ☐ No

If the answer to either of these questions is "Yes," see detailed instructions.

NATURE OF AUTHORSHIP Briefly describe nature of the material created by this author in which copyright is claimed. ▼

c

NAME OF AUTHOR ▼

DATES OF BIRTH AND DEATH
Year Born ▼   Year Died ▼

Was this contribution to the work a "work made for hire"?
- ☐ Yes
- ☐ No

AUTHOR'S NATIONALITY OR DOMICILE
Name of Country
OR { Citizen of ▶ _____
     Domiciled in ▶ _____

WAS THIS AUTHOR'S CONTRIBUTION TO THE WORK
Anonymous? ☐ Yes ☐ No
Pseudonymous? ☐ Yes ☐ No

If the answer to either of these questions is "Yes," see detailed instructions.

NATURE OF AUTHORSHIP Briefly describe nature of the material created by this author in which copyright is claimed. ▼

NOTE

Under the law, the "author" of a "work made for hire" is generally the employer, not the employee (see instructions). For any part of this work that was "made for hire" check "Yes" in the space provided, give the employer (or other person for whom the work was prepared) as "Author" of that part, and leave the space for dates of birth and death blank.

3

YEAR IN WHICH CREATION OF THIS WORK WAS COMPLETED This information must be given in all cases.

◀ Year

DATE AND NATION OF FIRST PUBLICATION OF THIS PARTICULAR WORK
Complete this information ONLY if this work has been published.
Month ▶ _____ Day ▶ _____ Year ▶ _____ ◀ Nation

4

COPYRIGHT CLAIMANT(S) Name and address must be given even if the claimant is the same as the author given in space 2.▼

See instructions before completing this space.

TRANSFER If the claimant(s) named here in space 4 are different from the author(s) named in space 2, give a brief statement of how the claimant(s) obtained ownership of the copyright.▼

DO NOT WRITE HERE OFFICE USE ONLY

APPLICATION RECEIVED

ONE DEPOSIT RECEIVED

TWO DEPOSITS RECEIVED

REMITTANCE NUMBER AND DATE

MORE ON BACK ▶
- Complete all applicable spaces (numbers 5-9) on the reverse side of this page.
- See detailed instructions.
- Sign the form at line 8.

DO NOT WRITE HERE

EXAMINED BY

CHECKED BY

☐ CORRESPONDENCE
Yes

☐ DEPOSIT ACCOUNT
FUNDS USED

FORM SR

FOR
COPYRIGHT
OFFICE
USE
ONLY

DO NOT WRITE ABOVE THIS LINE. IF YOU NEED MORE SPACE, USE A SEPARATE CONTINUATION SHEET.

PREVIOUS REGISTRATION Has registration for this work, or for an earlier version of this work, already been made in the Copyright Office?

☐ Yes ☐ No If your answer is "Yes," why is another registration being sought? (Check appropriate box) ▼

☐ This is the first published edition of a work previously registered in unpublished form.

☐ This is the first application submitted by this author as copyright claimant.

☐ This is a changed version of the work, as shown by space 6 on this application.

If your answer is "Yes," give: **Previous Registration Number** ▼   **Year of Registration** ▼

5

DERIVATIVE WORK OR COMPILATION Complete both space 6a & 6b for a derivative work; complete only 6b for a compilation.

a. Preexisting Material Identify any preexisting work or works that this work is based on or incorporates. ▼

b. Material Added to This Work Give a brief, general statement of the material that has been added to this work and in which copyright is claimed. ▼

6

See instructions
before completing
this space.

DEPOSIT ACCOUNT If the registration fee is to be charged to a Deposit Account established in the Copyright Office, give name and number of Account.

Name ▼   **Account Number** ▼

7

CORRESPONDENCE Give name and address to which correspondence about this application should be sent.   Name/Address/Apt/City/State/Zip ▼

Area Code & Telephone Number ▶

Be sure to
give your
daytime phone
◀ number.

CERTIFICATION* I, the undersigned, hereby certify that I am the

Check one ▼

☐ author

☐ other copyright claimant

☐ owner of exclusive right(s)

☐ authorized agent of _____
Name of author or other copyright claimant, or owner of exclusive right(s) ▲

of the work identified in this application and that the statements made
by me in this application are correct to the best of my knowledge.

Typed or printed name and date ▼ If this is a published work, this date must be the same as or later than the date of publication given in space 3.

_____ date ▶ _____

☞   Handwritten signature (X) ▼

8

**MAIL
CERTIFI-
CATE TO**

**Certificate
will be
mailed in
window
envelope**

Name ▼

Number/Street/Apartment Number ▼

City/State/ZIP ▼

Have you:
• Completed all necessary
  spaces?
• Signed your application in space
  8?
• Enclosed check or money order
  for $10 payable to *Register of
  Copyrights*?
• Enclosed your deposit material
  with the application and fee?

MAIL TO: Register of Copyrights,
Library of Congress, Washington,
D.C. 20559.

9

* 17 U.S.C. § 506(e): Any person who knowingly makes a false representation of a material fact in the application for copyright registration provided for by section 409 or in any written statement filed in
connection with the application, shall be fined not more than $2,500.

☆ U.S. GOVERNMENT PRINTING OFFICE: 1984—461-584/10,011

November 1984 — 100,000

APPLICATION
FOR
Renewal Registration

HOW TO REGISTER A RENEWAL CLAIM:

- **First:** Study the information on this page and make sure you know the answers to two questions:

  (1) What are the renewal time limits in your case?

  (2) Who can claim the renewal?

- **Second:** Turn this page over and read through the specific instructions for filling out Form RE. Make sure, before starting to complete the form, that the copyright is now eligible for renewal, that you are authorized to file a renewal claim, and that you have all of the information about the copyright you will need.

- **Third:** Complete all applicable spaces on Form RE, following the line-by-line instructions on the back of this page. Use typewriter, or print the information in dark ink.

- **Fourth:** Detach this sheet and send your completed Form RE to: Register of Copyrights, Library of Congress, Washington, D.C. 20559. Unless you have a Deposit Account in the Copyright Office, your application must be accompanied by a check or money order for $6, payable to: *Register of Copyrights*. Do not send copies, phonorecords, or supporting documents with your renewal application.

WHAT IS RENEWAL OF COPYRIGHT? For works originally copyrighted between January 1, 1950 and December 31, 1977, the statute now in effect provides for a first term of copyright protection lasting for 28 years, with the possibility of renewal for a second term of 47 years. If a valid renewal registration is made for a work, its total copyright term is 75 years (a first term of 28 years, plus a renewal term of 47 years). Example: in a work copyrighted in 1960, the first term will expire in 1988, but if renewed at the proper time the copyright will last through the end of 2035.

SOME BASIC POINTS ABOUT RENEWAL:

(1) There are strict time limits and deadlines for renewing a copyright.

(2) Only certain persons who fall into specific categories named in the law can claim renewal.

(3) The new copyright law does away with renewal requirements for works first copyrighted after 1977. However, copyrights that were already in their first copyright term on January 1, 1978 (that is, works originally copyrighted between January 1, 1950 and December 31, 1977) **will have to be renewed** in order to be protected for a second term.

TIME LIMITS FOR RENEWAL REGISTRATION: The new copyright statute provides that, in order to renew a copyright, the renewal application and fee must be received in the Copyright Office "within one year prior to the expiration of the copyright." It also provides that all terms of copyright will run through the end of the year in which they would otherwise expire. Since all copyright terms will expire on December 31st of their last year, all periods for renewal registration will run from December 31st of the 27th year of the copyright, and will end on December 31st of the following year.

To determine the time limits for renewal in your case:

(1) First, find out the date of original copyright for the work. (In the case of works originally registered in unpublished form, the date of copyright is the date of registration; for published works, copyright begins on the date of first publication.)

(2) Then add 28 years to the year the work was originally copyrighted.

Your answer will be the calendar year during which the copyright will be eligible for renewal, and December 31st of that year will be the renewal deadline. Example: a work originally copyrighted on April 19, 1957, will be eligible for renewal between December 31, 1984, and December 31, 1985.

WHO MAY CLAIM RENEWAL: Renewal copyright may be claimed only by those persons specified in the law. Except in the case of four specific types of works, the law gives the right to claim renewal to the individual author of the work, regardless of who owned the copyright during the original term. If the author is dead, the statute gives the right to claim renewal to certain of the author's beneficiaries (widow and children, executors, or next of kin, depending on the circumstances). The present owner (proprietor) of the copyright is entitled to claim renewal only in four specified cases, as explained in more detail on the reverse of this page.

CAUTION: Renewal registration is possible only if an acceptable application and fee are **received** in the Copyright Office during the renewal period and before the renewal deadline. If an acceptable application and fee are not received before the renewal deadline, the work falls into the public domain and the copyright cannot be renewed. The Copyright Office has no discretion to extend the renewal time limits.

PRIVACY ACT ADVISORY STATEMENT
Required by the Privacy Act of 1974 (Public Law 93-579)

AUTHORITY FOR REQUESTING THIS INFORMATION:
- Title 17, U.S.C., Sec. 304

FURNISHING THE REQUESTED INFORMATION IS:
- Voluntary

BUT IF THE INFORMATION IS NOT FURNISHED:
- It may be necessary to delay or refuse renewal registration

- If renewal registration is not made, the copyright will expire at the end of its 28th year

PRINCIPAL USES OF REQUESTED INFORMATION:
- Establishment and maintenance of a public record
- Examination of the application for compliance with legal requirements

OTHER ROUTINE USES:
- Public inspection and copying

- Preparation of public indexes
- Preparation of public catalogs of copyright registrations
- Preparation of search reports upon request

NOTE:
- No other advisory statement will be given you in connection with this application
- Please retain this statement and refer to it if we communicate with you regarding this application

INSTRUCTIONS FOR COMPLETING FORM RE

SPACE 1: RENEWAL CLAIM(S)

• **General Instructions:** In order for this application to result in a valid renewal, space 1 must identify one or more of the persons who are entitled to renew the copyright under the statute. Give the full name and address of each claimant, with a statement of the basis of each claim, using the wording given in these instructions.

• **Persons Entitled to Renew:**

A. The following persons may claim renewal in all types of works except those enumerated in Paragraph B, below:

1. The author, if living. State the claim as: *the author*.

2. The widow, widower, and/or children of the author, if the author is not living. State the claim as: *the widow (widower) of the author* . . . .
(Name of author)

and/or *the child (children) of the deceased author* . . . .
(Name of author)

3. The author's executor(s), if the author left a will and if there is no surviving widow, widower, or child. State the claim as: *the executor(s) of the author*
. . . .
(Name of author)

4. The next of kin of the author, if the author left no will and if there is no surviving widow, widower, or child. State the claim as: *the next of kin of the deceased author* . . . . *there being no will.*
(Name of author)

B. In the case of the following four types of works, the proprietor (owner of the copyright at the time of renewal registration) may claim renewal:

1. Posthumous work (a work as to which no copyright assignment or other contract for exploitation has occurred during the author's lifetime). State the claim as: *proprietor of copyright in a posthumous work.*

2. Periodical, cyclopedic, or other composite work. State the claim as: *proprietor of copyright in a composite work.*

3. "Work copyrighted by a corporate body otherwise than as assignee or licensee of the individual author." State the claim as: *proprietor of copyright in a work copyrighted by a corporate body otherwise than as assignee or licensee of the individual author.* (This type of claim is considered appropriate in relatively few cases.)

4. Work copyrighted by an employer for whom such work was made for hire. State the claim as: *proprietor of copyright in a work made for hire.*

SPACE 2: WORK RENEWED

• **General Instructions:** This space is to identify the particular work being renewed. The information given here should agree with that appearing in the certificate of original registration.

• **Title:** Give the full title of the work, together with any subtitles or descriptive wording included with the title in the original registration. In the case of a musical composition, give the specific instrumentation of the work.

• **Renewable Matter:** Copyright in a new version of a previous work (such as an arrangement, translation, dramatization, compilation, or work republished with new matter) covers only the additions, changes, or other new material appearing for the first time in that version. If this work was a new version, state in general the new matter upon which copyright was claimed.

• **Contribution to Periodical, Serial, or other Composite Work:** Separate renewal registration is possible for a work published as a contribution to a periodical, serial, or other composite work, whether the contribution was copyrighted independently or as part of the larger work in which it appeared. Each contribution published in a separate issue ordinarily requires a separate renewal registration. However, the new law provides an alternative, permitting groups of periodical contributions by the same individual author to be combined under a single renewal application and fee in certain cases.

If this renewal application covers a single contribution, give all of the requested information in space 2. If you are seeking to renew a group of contributions, include a reference such as "See space 5" in space 2 and give the requested information about all of the contributions in space 5.

SPACE 3: AUTHOR(S)

• **General Instructions:** The copyright secured in a new version of a work is independent of any copyright protection in material published earlier. The only "authors" of a new version are those who contributed copyrightable matter to it. Thus, for renewal purposes, the person who wrote the original version on which the new work is based cannot be regarded as an "author" of the new version, unless that person also contributed to the new matter.

• **Authors of Renewable Matter:** Give the full names of all authors who contributed copyrightable matter to this particular version of the work.

SPACE 4: FACTS OF ORIGINAL REGISTRATION

• **General Instructions:** Each item in space 4 should agree with the information appearing in the original registration for the work. If the work being renewed is a single contribution to a periodical or composite work that was not separately registered, give information about the particular issue in which the contribution appeared. You may leave this space blank if you are completing space 5.

• **Original Registration Number:** Give the full registration number, which is a series of numerical digits, preceded by one or more letters. The registration number appears in the upper right hand corner of the certificate of registration.

• **Original Copyright Claimant:** Give the name in which ownership of the copyright was claimed in the original registration.

• **Date of Publication or Registration:** Give only one date. If the original registration gave a publication date, it should be transcribed here; otherwise the registration was for an unpublished work, and the date of registration should be given.

SPACE 5: GROUP RENEWALS

• **General Instructions:** A single renewal registration can be made for a group of works if **all** of the following statutory conditions are met: (1) all of the works were written by the same author, who is named in space 3 and who is or was an individual (not an employer for hire); (2) all of the works were first published as contributions to periodicals (including newspapers) and were copyrighted on their first publication; (3) the renewal claimant or claimants, and the basis of claim or claims, as stated in space 1, is the same for all of the works; (4) the renewal application and fee are "received not more than 28 or less than 27 years after the 31st day of December of the calendar year in which all of the works were first published"; and (5) the renewal application identifies each work separately, including the periodical containing it and the date of first publication.

Time Limits for Group Renewals: To be renewed as a group, all of the contributions must have been first published during the same calendar year. For example, suppose six contributions by the same author were published on April 1, 1960, July 1, 1960, November 1, 1960, February 1, 1961, July 1, 1961, and March 1, 1962. The three 1960 copyrights can be combined and renewed at any time during 1988, and the two 1961 copyrights can be renewed as a group during 1989, but the 1962 copyright must be renewed by itself, in 1990.

Identification of Each Work: Give all of the requested information for each contribution. The registration number should be that for the contribution itself if it was separately registered, and the registration number for the periodical issue if it was not.

SPACES 6, 7 AND 8: FEE, MAILING INSTRUCTIONS, AND CERTIFICATION

• **Deposit Account and Mailing Instructions (Space 6):** If you maintain a Deposit Account in the Copyright Office, identify it in space 6. Otherwise, you will need to send the renewal registration fee of $6 with your form. The space headed "Correspondence" should contain the name and address of the person to be consulted if correspondence about the form becomes necessary

• **Certification (Space 7):** The renewal application is not acceptable unless it bears the handwritten signature of the renewal claimant or the duly authorized agent of the renewal claimant.

• **Address for Return of Certificate (Space 8):** The address box must be completed legibly, since the certificate will be returned in a window envelope.

FORM RE

UNITED STATES COPYRIGHT OFFICE

REGISTRATION NUMBER

EFFECTIVE DATE OF RENEWAL REGISTRATION

. . . .
(Month)   (Day)   (Year)

DO NOT WRITE ABOVE THIS LINE.   FOR COPYRIGHT OFFICE USE ONLY

(1)

Renewal Claimant(s)

RENEWAL CLAIMANT(S), ADDRESS(ES), AND STATEMENT OF CLAIM: (See Instructions)

1

Name . . . .

Address . . . .

Claiming as . . . .
(Use appropriate statement from instructions)

2

Name . . . .

Address . . . .

Claiming as . . . .
(Use appropriate statement from instructions)

3

Name . . . .

Address . . . .

Claiming as . . . .
(Use appropriate statement from instructions)

(2)

Work Renewed

TITLE OF WORK IN WHICH RENEWAL IS CLAIMED:

RENEWABLE MATTER:

CONTRIBUTION TO PERIODICAL OR COMPOSITE WORK:

Title of periodical or composite work: . . . .

If a periodical or other serial, give: Vol. . . . . No. . . . . Issue Date . . . .

(3)

Author(s)

AUTHOR(S) OF RENEWABLE MATTER:

(4)

Facts of Original Registration

ORIGINAL REGISTRATION NUMBER:

. . . .

ORIGINAL COPYRIGHT CLAIMANT:

ORIGINAL DATE OF COPYRIGHT:

• If the original registration for this work was made in published form, give:

DATE OF PUBLICATION: . . . .
(Month)   (Day)   (Year)

OR

• If the original registration for this work was made in unpublished form, give:

DATE OF REGISTRATION: . . . .
(Month)   (Day)   (Year)

EXAMINED BY:	RENEWAL APPLICATION RECEIVED:	FOR COPYRIGHT OFFICE USE ONLY
CHECKED BY:		
DEPOSIT ACCOUNT FUNDS USED: ☐	REMITTANCE NUMBER AND DATE:	

DO NOT WRITE ABOVE THIS LINE. FOR COPYRIGHT OFFICE USE ONLY

RENEWAL FOR GROUP OF WORKS BY SAME AUTHOR: To make a single registration for a group of works by the same individual author published as contributions to periodicals (see instructions), give full information about each contribution. If more space is needed, request continuation sheet (Form RE/CON).

⑤ Renewal for Group of Works

1
Title of Contribution: . . . .
Title of Periodical: . . . . Vol. . . . . No. . . . . Issue Date . . . .
Date of Publication: . . . . Registration Number: . . . .
(Month) (Day) (Year)

2
Title of Contribution: . . . .
Title of Periodical: . . . . Vol. . . . . No. . . . . Issue Date . . . .
Date of Publication: . . . . Registration Number: . . . .
(Month) (Day) (Year)

3
Title of Contribution: . . . .
Title of Periodical: . . . . Vol. . . . . No. . . . . Issue Date . . . .
Date of Publication: . . . . Registration Number: . . . .
(Month) (Day) (Year)

4
Title of Contribution: . . . .
Title of Periodical: . . . . Vol. . . . . No. . . . . Issue Date . . . .
Date of Publication: . . . . Registration Number: . . . .
(Month) (Day) (Year)

5
Title of Contribution: . . . .
Title of Periodical: . . . . Vol. . . . . No. . . . . Issue Date . . . .
Date of Publication: . . . . Registration Number: . . . .
(Month) (Day) (Year)

6
Title of Contribution: . . . .
Title of Periodical: . . . . Vol. . . . . No. . . . . Issue Date . . . .
Date of Publication: . . . . Registration Number: . . . .
(Month) (Day) (Year)

7
Title of Contribution: . . . .
Title of Periodical: . . . . Vol. . . . . No. . . . . Issue Date . . . .
Date of Publication: . . . . Registration Number: . . . .
(Month) (Day) (Year)

DEPOSIT ACCOUNT: (If the registration fee is to be charged to a Deposit Account established in the Copyright Office, give name and number of Account.)

Name: . . . .
Account Number: . . . .

CORRESPONDENCE: (Give name and address to which correspondence about this application should be sent.)

Name: . . . .
Address: . . . . (Apt.)
(City) (State) (ZIP)

⑥ Fee and Correspondence

CERTIFICATION: I, the undersigned, hereby certify that I am the: (Check one)
☐ renewal claimant   ☐ duly authorized agent of: . . . .
(Name of renewal claimant)
of the work identified in this application, and that the statements made by me in this application are correct to the best of my knowledge.

Handwritten signature: (X) . . . .

Typed or printed name: . . . .

Date: . . . .

⑦ Certification (Application must be signed)

MAIL CERTIFICATE TO

. . . .
(Name)
. . . .
(Number, Street and Apartment Number)
. . . .
(City) (State) (ZIP code)

(Certificate will be mailed in window envelope)

⑧ Address for Return of Certificate

☆ U.S. GOVERNMENT PRINTING OFFICE: 1978—261-022/10

Apr. 1978—500,000

USE THIS FORM WHEN:

- An earlier registration has been made in the Copyright Office; and

- Some of the facts given in that registration are incorrect or incomplete; and

- You want to place the correct or complete facts on record.

FORM CA
UNITED STATES COPYRIGHT OFFICE
LIBRARY OF CONGRESS
WASHINGTON, D.C. 20559

Application for
Supplementary Copyright Registration

To Correct or Amplify Information Given in the
Copyright Office Record of an Earlier Registration

What is "Supplementary Copyright Registration"? Supplementary registration is a special type of copyright registration provided for in section 408(d) of the copyright law.

Purpose of Supplementary Registration. As a rule, only one basic copyright registration can be made for the same work. To take care of cases where information in the basic registration turns out to be incorrect or incomplete, the law provides for "the filing of an application for supplementary registration, to correct an error in a copyright registration or to amplify the information given in a registration."

Earlier Registration Necessary. Supplementary registration can be made only if a basic copyright registration for the same work has already been completed.

Who May File. Once basic registration has been made for a work, any author or other copyright claimant, or owner of any exclusive right in the work, who wishes to correct or amplify the information given in the basic registration, may submit Form CA.

Please Note:

- Do not use Form CA to correct errors in statements on the copies or phonorecords of the work in question, or to reflect changes in the content of the work. If the work has been changed substantially, you should consider making an entirely new registration for the revised version to cover the additions or revisions.

- Do not use Form CA as a substitute for renewal registration. For works originally copyrighted between January 1, 1950 and December 31, 1977, registration of a renewal claim within strict time limits is necessary to extend the first 28-year copyright term to the full term of 75 years. This cannot be done by filing Form CA.

- Do not use Form CA as a substitute for recording a transfer of copyright or other document pertaining to rights under a copyright. Recording a document under section 205 of the statute gives all persons constructive notice of the facts stated in the document and may have other important consequences in cases of infringement or conflicting transfers. Supplementary registration does not have that legal effect.

How to Apply for Supplementary Registration:

First: Study the information on this page to make sure that filing an application on Form CA is the best procedure to follow in your case.

Second: Turn this page over and read through the specific instructions for filling out Form CA. Make sure, before starting to complete the form, that you have all of the detailed information about the basic registration you will need.

Third: Complete all applicable spaces on this form, following the line-by-line instructions on the back of this page. Use typewriter, or print the information in dark ink.

Fourth: Detach this sheet and send your completed Form CA to: Register of Copyrights, Library of Congress, Washington, D.C. 20559. Unless you have a Deposit Account in the Copyright Office, your application must be accompanied by a non-refundable filing fee in the form of a check or money order for $10 payable to: *Register of Copyrights.* Do not send copies, phonorecords, or supporting documents with your application, since they cannot be made part of the record of a supplementary registration.

What Happens When a Supplementary Registration is Made? When a supplementary registration is completed, the Copyright Office will assign it a new registration number in the appropriate registration category, and issue a certificate of supplementary registration under that number. The basic registration will not be expunged or cancelled, and the two registrations will both stand in the Copyright Office records. The supplementary registration will have the effect of calling the public's attention to a possible error or omission in the basic registration, and of placing the correct facts or the additional information on official record. Moreover, if the person on whose behalf Form CA is submitted is the same as the person identified as copyright claimant in the basic registration, the Copyright Office will place a note referring to the supplementary registration in its records of the basic registration.

PLEASE READ DETAILED INSTRUCTIONS ON REVERSE

Please read the following line-by-line instructions carefully and refer to them while completing Form CA.

INSTRUCTIONS
For Completing FORM CA (Supplementary Registration)

PART A: BASIC INSTRUCTIONS

• **General Instructions:** The information in this part identifies the basic registration to be corrected or amplified. Each item must agree exactly with the information as it already appears in the basic registration (even if the purpose of filing Form CA is to change one of these items).

• **Title of Work:** Give the title as it appears in the basic registration, including previous or alternative titles if they appear.

• **Registration Number:** This is a series of numerical digits, preceded by one or more letters. The registration number appears in the upper right hand corner of the certificate of registration.

• **Registration Date:** Give the year when the basic registration was completed.

• **Name(s) of Author(s) and Name(s) of Copyright Claimant(s):** Give all of the names as they appear in the basic registration.

PART B: CORRECTION

• **General Instructions:** Complete this part **only** if information in the basic registration was incorrect at the time that basic registration was made. Leave this part blank and complete Part C, instead, if your purpose is to add, update, or clarify information rather than to rectify an actual error.

• **Location and Nature of Incorrect Information:** Give the line number and the heading or description of the space in the basic registration where the error occurs (for example: "Line number 3 . . . Citizenship of author").

• **Incorrect Information as it Appears in Basic Registration:** Transcribe the erroneous statement exactly as it appears in the basic registration.

• **Corrected Information:** Give the statement as it should have appeared.

• **Explanation of Correction (Optional):** If you wish, you may add an explanation of the error or its correction.

PART C: AMPLIFICATION

• **General Instructions:** Complete this part if you want to provide any of the following: (1) additional information that could have been given but was omitted at the time of basic registration; (2) changes in facts, such as changes of title or address of claimant, that have occurred since the basic registration; or (3) explanations clarifying information in the basic registration.

• **Location and Nature of Information to be Amplified:** Give the line number and the heading or description of the space in the basic registration where the information to be amplified appears.

• **Amplified Information:** Give a statement of the added, updated, or explanatory information as clearly and succinctly as possible.

• **Explanation of Amplification (Optional):** If you wish, you may add an explanation of the amplification.

PARTS D, E, F, G: CONTINUATION, FEE, MAILING INSTRUCTIONS AND CERTIFICATION

• **Continuation (Part D):** Use this space if you do not have enough room in Parts B or C.

• **Deposit Account and Mailing Instructions (Part E):** If you maintain a Deposit Account in the Copyright Office, identify it in Part E. Otherwise, you will need to send the non-refundable filing fee of $10 with your form. The space headed "Correspondence" should contain the name and address of the person to be consulted if correspondence about the form becomes necessary.

• **Certification (Part F):** The application is not acceptable unless it bears the handwritten signature of the author, or other copyright claimant, or of the owner of exclusive right(s), or of the duly authorized agent of such author, claimant, or owner.

• **Address for Return of Certificate (Part G):** The address box must be completed legibly, since the certificate will be returned in a window envelope.

PRIVACY ACT ADVISORY STATEMENT
Required by the Privacy Act of 1974 (Public Law 93-579)

AUTHORITY FOR REQUESTING THIS INFORMATION:
• Title 17, U.S.C., Sec. 408 (d)

FURNISHING THE REQUESTED INFORMATION IS:
• Voluntary

BUT IF THE INFORMATION IS NOT PROVIDED:
• It may be necessary to delay or refuse supplementary registration

PRINCIPAL USES OF REQUESTED INFORMATION:
• Establishment and maintenance of a public record
• Evaluation for compliance with legal requirements

OTHER ROUTINE USES:
• Public inspection and copying
• Preparation of public indexes

• Preparation of public catalogs of copyright registrations
• Preparation of search reports upon request

NOTE:
• No other Advisory Statement will be given you in connection with the application
• Please retain this statement and refer to it if we communicate with you regarding this application

FORM CA
UNITED STATES COPYRIGHT OFFICE

REGISTRATION NUMBER

| TX | TXU | PA | PAU | VA | VAU | SR | SRU | RE |

Effective Date of Supplementary Registration

. . . .
MONTH   DAY   YEAR

DO NOT WRITE ABOVE THIS LINE. FOR COPYRIGHT OFFICE USE ONLY

(A) Basic Instructions

TITLE OF WORK:

REGISTRATION NUMBER OF BASIC REGISTRATION:

YEAR OF BASIC REGISTRATION:

NAME(S) OF AUTHOR(S):

NAME(S) OF COPYRIGHT CLAIMANT(S):

(B) Correction

LOCATION AND NATURE OF INCORRECT INFORMATION IN BASIC REGISTRATION:

Line Number . . . . Line Heading or Description . . . .

INCORRECT INFORMATION AS IT APPEARS IN BASIC REGISTRATION:

CORRECTED INFORMATION:

EXPLANATION OF CORRECTION: (Optional)

(C) Amplification

LOCATION AND NATURE OF INFORMATION IN BASIC REGISTRATION TO BE AMPLIFIED:

Line Number . . . . Line Heading or Description . . . .

AMPLIFIED INFORMATION:

EXPLANATION OF AMPLIFIED INFORMATION: (Optional)

EXAMINED BY:	FORM CA RECEIVED:	FOR COPYRIGHT OFFICE USE ONLY
CHECKED BY:.		
CORRESPONDENCE: ☐ YES	REMITTANCE NUMBER AND DATE:	
REFERENCE TO THIS REGISTRATION ADDED TO BASIC REGISTRATION: ☐ YES ☐ NO	DEPOSIT ACCOUNT FUNDS USED: ☐	

DO NOT WRITE ABOVE THIS LINE. FOR COPYRIGHT OFFICE USE ONLY

CONTINUATION OF: (Check which) ☐ PART B OR ☐ PART C

D
Continuation

DEPOSIT ACCOUNT: If the registration fee is to be charged to a Deposit Account established in the Copyright Office, give name and number of Account:

Name . . . . Account Number . . . .

CORRESPONDENCE: Give name and address to which correspondence should be sent:

Name . . . . Apt. No. . . . .

Address . . . .
　　　　　　(Number and Street)　　　　　　　　　(City)　　　　(State)　　　　(ZIP Code)

E
Deposit Account and Mailing Instructions

CERTIFICATION ✱ I, the undersigned, hereby certify that I am the: (Check one)

☐ author ☐ other copyright claimant ☐ owner of exclusive right(s) ☐ authorized agent of: . . . .
　　　　　　　　　　　　　　　　　　　　　　(Name of author or other copyright claimant, or owner of exclusive right(s))

of the work identified in this application and that the statements made by me in this application are correct to the best of my knowledge.

☞ Handwritten signature: (X) . . . .

Typed or printed name. . . . .

Date: . . . .

✱ 17 USC §506(e): FALSE REPRESENTATION—Any person who knowingly makes a false representation of a material fact in the application for copyright registration provided for by section 409, or in any written statement filed in connection with the application, shall be fined not more than $2,500.

F
Certification (Application must be signed)

. . . .
(Name)

. . . .
(Number, Street and Apartment Number)

. . . .
(City)　　　(State)　　(ZIP code)

MAIL CERTIFICATE TO

(Certificate will be mailed in window envelope)

G
Address for Return of Certificate

July 1986—20,000

☆U.S. GOVERNMENT PRINTING OFFICE: 1986: 491–560/40,00

THIS FORM:

- Can be used solely as an adjunct to a basic application for copyright registration.
- Is not acceptable unless submitted together with Form TX, Form PA, or Form VA.
- Is acceptable only if the group of works listed on it all qualify for a single copyright registration under 17 U.S.C. § 408 (c)(2).

FORM GR/CP

UNITED STATES COPYRIGHT OFFICE
LIBRARY OF CONGRESS
WASHINGTON, D.C. 20559

ADJUNCT APPLICATION
for Copyright Registration for a Group of Contributions to Periodicals

WHEN TO USE FORM GR/CP: Form GR/CP is the appropriate adjunct application form to use when you are submitting a basic application on Form TX, Form PA, or Form VA, for a group of works that qualify for a single registration under section 408(c)(2) of the copyright statute.

WHEN DOES A GROUP OF WORKS QUALIFY FOR A SINGLE REGISTRATION UNDER 17 U.S.C. §408 (c)(2)? The statute provides that a single copyright registration for a group of works can be made if **all** of the following conditions are met:

(1) All of the works are by the same author, who is an individual (not an employer for hire); and

(2) All of the works were first published as contributions to periodicals (including newspapers) within a twelve-month period; and

(3) Each of the contributions as first published bore a separate copyright notice, and the name of the owner of copyright in the work (or an abbreviation or alternative designation of the owner) was the same in each notice; and

(4) One copy of the entire periodical issue or newspaper section in which each contribution was first published must be deposited with the application; and

(5) The application must identify each contribution separately, including the periodical containing it and the date of its first publication.

How to Apply for Group Registration:

First: Study the information on this page to make sure that all of the works you want to register together as a group qualify for a single registration.

Second: Turn this page over and read through the detailed instructions for group registration. Decide which form you should use for the basic registration (Form TX for nondramatic literary works; or Form PA for musical, dramatic, and other works of the performing arts; or Form VA for pictorial and graphic works). Be sure that you have all of the information you need before you start filling out both the basic and the adjunct application forms.

Third: Complete the basic application form, following the detailed instructions accompanying it **and the special instructions on the reverse of this page**.

Fourth: Complete the adjunct application on Form GR/CP and mail it, together with the basic application form and the required copy of each contribution, to: Register of Copyrights, Library of Congress, Washington, D.C. 20559. Unless you have a Deposit Account in the Copyright Office, your application and copies must be accompanied by a check or money order for $10, payable to: *Register of Copyrights.*

PROCEDURE FOR GROUP REGISTRATION

TWO APPLICATION FORMS MUST BE FILED

When you apply for a single registration to cover a group of contributions to periodicals, you must submit two application forms:

(1) A basic application on either Form TX, or Form PA, or Form VA. It must contain all of the information required for copyright registration except the titles and information concerning publication of the contributions.

(2) An adjunct application on Form GR/CP. The purpose of this form is to provide separate identification for each of the contributions and to give information about their first publication, as required by the statute.

WHICH BASIC APPLICATION FORM TO USE

The basic application form you choose to submit should be determined by the nature of the contributions you are registering. As long as they meet the statutory qualifications for group registration (outlined on the reverse of this page), the contributions can be registered together even if they are entirely different in nature, type, or content. However, you must choose which of three forms is generally the most appropriate on which to submit your basic application:

Form TX: for nondramatic literary works consisting primarily of text. Examples are fiction, verse, articles, news stories, features, essays, reviews, editorials, columns, quizzes, puzzles, and advertising copy.

Form PA: for works of the performing arts. Examples are music, drama, choreography, and pantomimes.

Form VA: for works of the visual arts. Examples are photographs, drawings, paintings, prints, art reproductions, cartoons, comic strips, charts, diagrams, maps, pictorial ornamentation, and pictorial or graphic material published as advertising.

If your contributions differ in nature, choose the form most suitable for the majority of them. However, if any of the contributions consists preponderantly of nondramatic text matter in English, you should file Form TX for the entire group. This is because Form TX is the only form containing spaces for information about the manufacture of copies, which the statute requires to be given for certain works.

REGISTRATION FEE FOR GROUP REGISTRATION

The fee for registration of a group of contributions to periodicals is $10, no matter how many contributions are listed on Form GR/CP. Unless you maintain a Deposit Account in the Copyright Office, the registration fee must accompany your application forms and copies. Make your remittance payable to: *Register of Copyrights*.

WHAT COPIES SHOULD BE DEPOSITED FOR GROUP REGISTRATION?

The application forms you file for group registration must be accompanied by one complete copy of each contribution listed in Form GR/CP, exactly as the contribution was first published in a periodical. The deposit must consist of the entire issue of the periodical containing the contribution; or, if the contribution was first published in a newspaper, the deposit should consist of the entire section in which the contribution appeared. Tear sheets or proof copies are not acceptable for deposit.

COPYRIGHT NOTICE REQUIREMENTS

For published works, the law provides that a copyright notice in a specified form "shall be placed on all publicly distributed copies from which the work can be visually perceived." The required form of the notice generally consists of three elements: (1) the symbol "©", or the word "Copyright", or the abbreviation "Copr."; (2) the year of first publication of the work; and (3) the name of the owner of copyright in the work, or an abbreviation or alternative form of the name. For example: "© 1978 Samuel Craig".

Among the conditions for group registration of contributions to periodicals, the statute establishes two requirements involving the copyright notice:

(1) Each of the contributions as first published must have borne a separate copyright notice; and

(2) "The name of the owner of copyright in the work, or an abbreviation by which the name can be recognized, or a generally known alternative designation of the owner" must have been the same in each notice.

HOW TO FILL OUT THE BASIC APPLICATION FORM WHEN APPLYING FOR GROUP REGISTRATION

In general, the instructions for filling out the basic application (Form TX, Form PA, or Form VA) apply to group registrations. In addition, please observe the following specific instructions:

Space 1 (Title): Do not give information concerning any of the contributions in space 1 of the basic application. Instead, in the block headed "Title of this Work", state: "See Form GR/CP, attached". Leave the other blocks in space 1 blank.

Space 2 (Author): Give the name and other information concerning the author of all of the contributions listed in Form GR/CP. To qualify for group registration, all of the contributions must have been written by the same individual author.

Space 3 (Creation and Publication): In the block calling for the year of creation, give the year of creation of the last of the contributions to be completed. Leave the block calling for the date and nation of first publication blank.

Space 4 (Claimant): Give all of the requested information, which must be the same for all of the contributions listed on Form GR/CP.

Other spaces: Complete all of the applicable spaces, and be sure that the form is signed in the certification space.

HOW TO FILL OUT FORM GR/CP

PART A: IDENTIFICATION OF APPLICATION

• **Identification of Basic Application:** Indicate, by checking one of the boxes, which of the basic application forms (Form TX, or Form PA, or Form VA) you are filing for registration.

• **Identification of Author and Claimant:** Give the name of the individual author exactly as it appears in line 2 of the basic application, and give the name of the copyright claimant exactly as it appears in line 4. These must be the same for all of the contributions listed in Part B of Form GR/CP.

PART B: REGISTRATION FOR GROUP OF CONTRIBUTIONS

• **General Instructions:** Under the statute, a group of contributions to periodicals will qualify for a single registration only if the application "identifies each work separately, including the periodical containing it and its date of first publication." Part B of the Form GR/CP provides lines enough to list 19 separate contributions; if you need more space, use additional Forms GR/CP. If possible, list the contributions in the order of their publication, giving the earliest first. Number each line consecutively.

• **Important:** All of the contributions listed on Form GR/CP must have been published within a single twelve-month period. This does not mean that all of the contributions must have been published during the same calendar year, but it does mean that, to be grouped in a single application, the earliest and latest contributions must not have been published more than twelve months apart. Example: Contributions published on April 1, 1978, July 1, 1978, and March 1, 1979, could be grouped together, but a contribution published on April 15, 1979, could not be registered with them as part of the group.

• **Title of Contribution:** Each contribution must be given a title that is capable of identifying that particular work and of distinguishing it from others. If the contribution as published in the periodical bears a title (or an identifying phrase that could serve as a title), transcribe its wording completely and exactly.

• **Identification of Periodical:** Give the over-all title of the periodical in which the contribution was first published, together with the volume and issue number (if any) and the issue date.

• **Pages:** Give the number of the page of the periodical issue on which the contribution appeared. If the contribution covered more than one page, give the inclusive pages, if possible.

• **First Publication:** The statute defines "publication" as "the distribution of copies or phonorecords of a work to the public by sale or other transfer of ownership, or by rental, lease, or lending"; a work is also "published" if there has been an "offering to distribute copies or phonorecords to a group of persons for purposes of further distribution, public performance, or public display." Give the full date (month, day, and year) when, and the country where, publication of the periodical issue containing the contribution first occurred. If first publication took place simultaneously in the United States and other countries, it is sufficient to state "U.S.A."

NOTE: The advantage of group registration is that it allows any number of works published within a twelve-month period to be registered "on the basis of a single deposit, application, and registration fee." On the other hand, group registration may also have disadvantages under certain circumstances. If infringement of a published work begins before the work has been registered, the copyright owner can still obtain the ordinary remedies for copyright infringement (including injunctions, actual damages and profits, and impounding and disposition of infringing articles). However, in that situation—where the copyright in a published work is infringed before registration is made—the owner cannot obtain special remedies (statutory damages and attorney's fees) unless registration was made within three months after first publication of the work.

ADJUNCT APPLICATION
for
Copyright Registration for a Group of Contributions to Periodicals

- Use this adjunct form only if your are making a single registration for a group of contributions to periodicals, and you are also filing a basic application on Form TX, Form PA, or Form VA. Follow the instructions, attached.
- Number each line in Part B consecutively. Use additional Forms GR/CP if you need more space.
- Submit this adjunct form with the basic application form. Clip (do not tape or staple) and fold all sheets together before submitting them.

FORM GR/CP
UNITED STATES COPYRIGHT OFFICE

REGISTRATION NUMBER
TX   PA   VA

EFFECTIVE DATE OF REGISTRATION
. . . .
(Month)   (Day)   (Year)

FORM GR/CP RECEIVED

Page _____ of _____ pages

DO NOT WRITE ABOVE THIS LINE. FOR COPYRIGHT OFFICE USE ONLY

Ⓐ

Identification of Application

IDENTIFICATION OF BASIC APPLICATION:
- This application for copyright registration for a group of contributions to periodicals is submitted as an adjunct to an application filed on: (Check which)

     ☐ Form TX   ☐ Form PA   ☐ Form VA

IDENTIFICATION OF AUTHOR AND CLAIMANT: (Give the name of the author and the name of the copyright claimant in all of the contributions listed in Part B of this form. The names should be the same as the names given in spaces 2 and 4 of the basic application.)

Name of Author: . . . .

Name of Copyright Claimant: . . . .

Ⓑ

Registration For Group of Contributions

COPYRIGHT REGISTRATION FOR A GROUP OF CONTRIBUTIONS TO PERIODICALS: (To make a single registration for a group of works by the same individual author, all first published as contributions to periodicals within a 12-month period (see instructions), give full information about each contribution. If more space is needed, use additional Forms GR/CP.)

☐ Title of Contribution: . . . .
    Title of Periodical: . . . . Vol. . . . . No. . . . . Issue Date . . . . Pages . . . .
    Date of First Publication: . . . . Nation of First Publication . . . .
    (Month) (Day) (Year)   (Country)

☐ Title of Contribution: . . . .
    Title of Periodical: . . . . Vol. . . . . No. . . . . Issue Date . . . . Pages . . . .
    Date of First Publication: . . . . Nation of First Publication . . . .
    (Month) (Day) (Year)   (Country)

☐ Title of Contribution: . . . .
    Title of Periodical: . . . . Vol. . . . . No. . . . . Issue Date . . . . Pages . . . .
    Date of First Publication: . . . . Nation of First Publication . . . .
    (Month) (Day) (Year)   (Country)

☐ Title of Contribution: . . . .
    Title of Periodical: . . . . Vol. . . . . No. . . . . Issue Date . . . . Pages . . . .
    Date of First Publication: . . . . Nation of First Publication . . . .
    (Month) (Day) (Year)   (Country)

☐ Title of Contribution: . . . .
    Title of Periodical: . . . . Vol. . . . . No. . . . . Issue Date . . . . Pages . . . .
    Date of First Publication: . . . . Nation of First Publication . . . .
    (Month) (Day) (Year)   (Country)

☐ Title of Contribution: . . . .
    Title of Periodical: . . . . Vol. . . . . No. . . . . Issue Date . . . . Pages . . . .
    Date of First Publication: . . . . Nation of First Publication . . . .
    (Month) (Day) (Year)   (Country)

☐ Title of Contribution: . . . .
    Title of Periodical: . . . . Vol. . . . . No. . . . . Issue Date . . . . Pages . . . .
    Date of First Publication: . . . . Nation of First Publication . . . .
    (Month) (Day) (Year)   (Country)

☐ Title of Contribution: ....
Title of Periodical: .... Vol. ..... No. ..... Issue Date .... Pages ....
Date of First Publication: .... Nation of First Publication ....
(Month)   (Day)   (Year)   (Country)

B
Continued

☐ Title of Contribution: ....
Title of Periodical: .... Vol. ..... No. ..... Issue Date .... Pages ....
Date of First Publication: .... Nation of First Publication ....
(Month)   (Day)   (Year)   (Country)

☐ Title of Contribution: ....
Title of Periodical: .... Vol. ..... No. ..... Issue Date .... Pages ....
Date of First Publication: .... Nation of First Publication ....
(Month)   (Day)   (Year)   (Country)

☐ Title of Contribution: ....
Title of Periodical: .... Vol. ..... No. ..... Issue Date .... Pages ....
Date of First Publication: .... Nation of First Publication ....
(Month)   (Day)   (Year)   (Country)

☐ Title of Contribution: ....
Title of Periodical: .... Vol. ..... No. ..... Issue Date .... Pages ....
Date of First Publication: .... Nation of First Publication ....
(Month)   (Day)   (Year)   (Country)

☐ Title of Contribution: ....
Title of Periodical: .... Vol. ..... No. ..... Issue Date .... Pages ....
Date of First Publication: .... Nation of First Publication ....
(Month)   (Day)   (Year)   (Country)

☐ Title of Contribution: ....
Title of Periodical: .... Vol. ..... No. ..... Issue Date .... Pages ....
Date of First Publication: .... Nation of First Publication ....
(Month)   (Day)   (Year)   (Country)

☐ Title of Contribution: ....
Title of Periodical: .... Vol. ..... No. ..... Issue Date .... Pages ....
Date of First Publication: .... Nation of First Publication ....
(Month)   (Day)   (Year)   (Country)

☐ Title of Contribution: ....
Title of Periodical: .... Vol. ..... No. ..... Issue Date .... Pages ....
Date of First Publication: .... Nation of First Publication ....
(Month)   (Day)   (Year)   (Country)

☐ Title of Contribution: ....
Title of Periodical: .... Vol. ..... No. ..... Issue Date .... Pages ....
Date of First Publication: .... Nation of First Publication ....
(Month)   (Day)   (Year)   (Country)

☐ Title of Contribution: ....
Title of Periodical: .... Vol. ..... No. ..... Issue Date .... Pages ....
Date of First Publication: .... Nation of First Publication ....
(Month)   (Day)   (Year)   (Country)

☐ Title of Contribution: ....
Title of Periodical: .... Vol. ..... No. ..... Issue Date .... Pages ....
Date of First Publication: .... Nation of First Publication ....
(Month)   (Day)   (Year)   (Country)

NOTES

NOTES

NOTES

NOTES

NOTES

NOTES

NOTES

NOTES